The Prayer Life

Andrew Murray

Modern English Edition

First published in 1913

Note: while the original material is public domain, this modern translation of it is NOT public domain and is copyright of Pastor Joe Lighthall, 2025.

All rights reserved.

Permission is required for reuse, reproduction, or distribution of this translated edition.

ISBN 978-1-918219-49-4

This modern edition first published: December 2025

Published by: Cosmic Jive Publishing
www.cosmicjivepublishing.com

For permissions and inquiries, contact:
info@cosmicjivepublishing.com

About This Edition

Andrew Murray's writings have long been cherished as classics of Christian devotion, yet many readers today find them difficult to approach. His rich vocabulary, lengthy sentences, dense paragraphs, and use of outdated English can create real barriers—even for those fluent in the language or trained in theology.

Every chapter, section, and biblical quotation appears in the same order as the original. Nothing has been added, removed, or softened. What has changed is only the presentation. The Victorian-era language has been carefully rewritten in clear, contemporary English so readers can immediately grasp Murray's full message. Roman numerals have been replaced with standard numbers, long sentences and paragraphs have been shortened for readability,.

This work of modernization is simply an effort to remove anything that might keep modern readers from hearing Murray clearly. His teaching then becomes not only understandable, but gripping, grounded, deeply practical, and profoundly moving

Murray wrote with a rare blend of humility, passion, and spiritual authority forged in a lifetime of communion with God. When his words are presented in fresh, accessible English, their light shines even more brightly.

My hope is that this edition will open the way for many who long to draw from Murray's wisdom but have felt hindered before by the language of another era. May these pages awaken in you a renewed hunger for prayer and a deeper desire to spend time alone with God.

Pastor Joe Lighthall, 2025

INTRODUCTION

A few words about how this book came to be written will help you understand its message more clearly.

This book grew out of a ministers' conference held in Stellenbosch, South Africa, in April 1912.

Before the conference, Professor de Vos from our Theological Seminary wrote a letter to all the ministers of our Church (the Dtch Reformed Church). In it, he spoke about the poor spiritual condition, found in general, of the worldwide Church, across all denominations. He said we needed to ask honestly how much this same weakness existed among us.

Professor de Vos believed there was no question that spiritual power was lacking. He said it was essential that we come together before God and seek out the true cause of the problem.

He wrote that if we're honest with ourselves, we must admit that our unbelief and our sin are the reason for this lack of spiritual power among us. It makes us guilty before God. It is nothing less than grieving the Holy Spirit.

His invitation received a strong response. All four of our theology professors joined more than two hundred ministers, missionaries, and students. His letter set the tone for the entire conference. From the very beginning, it became clear that confession was the only path toward real repentance and restoration.

Later in the conference, everyone was invited to speak about the sins they believed were weakening the Church. At first, some people began pointing out the failures they had noticed in other ministers—in their behavior, their beliefs, or their work.

But we quickly realized this was not the right approach. Each person needed to recognize their own guilt.

In His kindness, the Lord led us to see that prayerlessness was one of the deepest roots of the Church's weakness. No one could say they were free from this sin.

Nothing shows a weak spiritual life—whether in a minister or a congregation—more clearly than a lack of steady, faithful prayer.

Prayer is the heartbeat of spiritual life. It is the channel through which God pours out His blessing and power on both ministers and people.

Consistent, believing, persevering prayer always brings strength and abundance.

As confession began to take place among us, a question naturally surfaced: Can we really expect to overcome everything that has hindered our prayer life in the past?

In earlier, smaller gatherings, many had longed for a fresh beginning. But they lacked the courage to believe they could sustain the kind of prayer life they saw in Scripture.

They had tried before and failed. They couldn't bring themselves to promise God that they would live and pray as He desired. It felt impossible to them.

These confessions slowly led us to a great truth: The only power for a new prayer life comes from a new, deeper relationship with our Savior.

When we see Him as the One who saves us from all sin—including the sin of prayerlessness—and when we surrender in faith to closer fellowship with Him, His love begins to shape our lives. And in that life of love, prayer becomes the natural expression of the soul.

Before the conference ended, many were able to say they were going home with new light and new hope. In Jesus Christ, they had found the strength for a new beginning in prayer.

—A.M., 1913

1

THE SIN AND CAUSE OF PRAYERLESSNESS

If our conscience is going to speak honestly—and if our hearts are really going to feel sorrow for their sin—each of us must name our sin directly. Confession has to be personal.

In a gathering of ministers, there is probably no single sin we should acknowledge with deeper shame than prayerlessness. We really are all guilty of it.

Why is prayerlessness such a serious sin?

At first, it may seem like just a weakness. We blame lack of time or constant distractions, and because of this, we fail to see how serious the problem really is. But we must be honest now. From this point forward, we need to recognize prayerlessness as the sin it truly is.

PRAYERLESSNESS DISHONORS GOD

God—holy, glorious, and loving—invites us to come to Him. He wants us to talk with Him, ask for what we need, and find joy in fellowship with Him.

He created us so our greatest purpose, joy, and salvation would be found in Him.

Yet how do we treat this heavenly privilege?

Many people spend only a few minutes in prayer. They say they don't have time. They say they don't feel like praying. They can't imagine spending even half an hour with God.

It's not that they never pray—they do. But there is no joy in it. Their prayer life doesn't show that God is their greatest treasure.

If a friend wants to visit them, they find time for that. They rearrange their schedule, even at personal cost, simply to talk with their friend. So clearly, people make time for what truly matters to them. But they say they "cannot" make time to enjoy fellowship with God.

They make time for anyone who might help them, yet day after day, month after month goes by without them spending even one hour alone with Him.

Doesn't this show how deeply God is dishonored? How easily we place everything else ahead of Him?

When we finally see this sin for what it is, we will cry out in shame: "Lord, have mercy on me and forgive this terrible sin of prayerlessness."

Prayerlessness Weakens Spiritual Life

Prayerlessness shows that for most people, life is still shaped by the flesh rather than the Spirit. Prayer is the pulse of spiritual life. Just as a doctor checks the pulse to know the condition of the heart, prayer reveals the condition of our inner life with God.

Prayerlessness shows that, for many Christians and ministers, the life of God within them is dangerously weak.

People often complain that the Church fails to fulfill her calling—that she fails to influence her members, fails to free them from the world's grip, and fails to lead them into lives truly dedicated to God.

People also speak about the Church's lack of concern for the millions who do not yet know Christ, though He entrusted the lost to us so we could share His love and salvation with them.

Why don't thousands of Christian workers have more spiritual impact? There is only one real reason: their work is prayerless.

With all their effort in study, ministry, preaching, and conversation, they still lack the steady, believing prayer that draws down the power of the Spirit from above.

It is this sin of prayerlessness that drains spiritual life of its strength.

How the Church Loses Out Because of Prayerless Ministers

A minister's calling is to lead believers into a life of prayer. But how can he do that if he barely knows how to talk with God himself? If he does not receive fresh grace each day from the Holy Spirit for his own life and work?

A minister cannot lead people higher than he has gone. He cannot passionately point them toward a life he is not living.

Thousands of Christians know almost nothing of the blessing that comes from real fellowship with God in prayer.

Many know something of it and long for more, yet they rarely hear persistent encouragement from the pulpit urging them to seek this blessing until they experience it.

The reason is simple: the minister knows too little of the power of prayer, so prayer does not have the central place in his ministry that God intends.

What a transformation we would see in our congregations if ministers truly recognized the sin of prayerlessness—and were freed from it!

The Impossibility of Preaching the Gospel to All People

We cannot fulfill Christ's command to take the gospel to all people as long as the sin of prayerlessness remains unaddressed and unchanged.

Many believe that missions desperately need men and women who will fully give themselves to the Lord and labor in prayer for the salvation of souls.

It has often been said that God is ready and willing to bless and rescue the world He has redeemed—if only His people were willing, and if only they would cry out to Him day and night in prayer.

But how can congregations be moved to that kind of prayer unless ministers themselves are first transformed? Ministers must recognize that the most essential part of their calling is not preaching, visiting, or running church activities—but fellowship with God in prayer until they are clothed with power from on high.

Let everything we think, plan, and hope for in God's kingdom drive us to acknowledge the sin of prayerlessness.

May God help us root it out.

May He free us from it through the blood and power of Christ Jesus.

May He teach every minister to see the glorious place he can stand in once he is set free from this root sin. Then —strengthened with courage and joy, in faith and perseverance—he can move forward with his God.

May the Lord press the weight of the sin of prayerlessness on our hearts so deeply that we cannot rest until it is removed from us through the name and power of Jesus. And He will make this possible.

A Witness from America

In 1898, two members of a New York Presbytery attended the Northfield Conference, a gathering focused on deepening spiritual life. They returned to their work with renewed enthusiasm and began encouraging revival throughout the entire Presbytery.

At one of their meetings, the chairman felt led to ask the ministers a question about their prayer habits.

"Brothers," he said, "let's confess before God and before one another today. It will do us good. Will everyone who spends at least half an hour every day with God in connection with his work please raise a hand?"

One hand went up.

He continued: "All who spend fifteen minutes—raise your hand."

Not even half the hands were raised.

Then he said, "Prayer—the working power of Christ's Church—and half the workers barely use it. All who spend five minutes, raise your hands."

Every hand went up.

Later, one man privately admitted he wasn't even sure he spent five minutes a day in prayer.

"It's an awful revelation," he said. "It shows how little time I really spend with God."

THE CAUSE OF PRAYERLESSNESS

At an elders' prayer meeting, a brother asked, "What causes so much prayerlessness? Isn't the real issue unbelief?"

The reply was, "Yes—but then we must ask another question: what causes that unbelief?"

When the disciples asked Jesus why they couldn't cast out the demon, He answered, "Because of your unbelief." But He also added, "This kind does not go out except by prayer and fasting" (Matthew 17:19–21).

If our lives are not marked by self-denial—letting go of the world—and by prayer that reaches toward heaven, then our faith has no foundation.

A life ruled by the flesh instead of the Spirit is the true root of the prayerlessness we complain about.

As we left the meeting, a brother said to me, "That's the whole issue. We want to pray in the Spirit while still living according to the flesh. And that's impossible."

If someone seeks healing, the first step is always to identify the real cause of the sickness. If we misdiagnose the cause, true healing is impossible.

In the same way, we must clearly understand the cause of our spiritual deadness and our failure in prayer. The inner room of prayer should be a place of blessing. We need to recognize the real root of the problem.

Scripture teaches that there are only two ways a Christian can live: according to the Spirit or according to the flesh. These two powers oppose each other completely.

This is where many Christians struggle. They are truly born again by the Spirit and have received God's life, but their daily living is shaped not by the Spirit but by the flesh.

Paul wrote to the Galatians, "Are you so foolish? Having begun in the Spirit, are you now being perfected by the flesh?" (Galatians 3:3).

Their service to God was controlled by outward performance rather than the Spirit. And when the flesh directs our service, it inevitably leads to sin. So Paul lists not only serious sins like adultery, murder, and drunkenness as works of the flesh, but also everyday sins like anger, arguments, and conflict.

He commands, "Walk in the Spirit, and you will not fulfill the desires of the flesh... If we live in the Spirit, let us also walk in the Spirit" (Galatians 5:16, 25).

The Spirit must be honored not only as the giver of new life, but as the leader and guide of our entire way of living. Otherwise, we remain what Scripture calls "carnal."

Many Christians understand little about this. They don't

grasp the deep sinfulness of the flesh and unknowingly give in to it.

"God condemned sin in the flesh" (Romans 8:3)—on Christ's cross.

"Those who belong to Christ have crucified the flesh with its passions and desires" (Galatians 5:24).

The flesh cannot be improved or made holy.

"The carnal mind is hostile to God. It does not submit to God's law, and it cannot" (Romans 8:7).

The only way to deal with the flesh is the way Christ dealt with it: by bringing it to the cross.

"Our old self was crucified with Him" (Romans 6:6). By faith, we do the same—we treat the flesh each day as something condemned, something that belongs on the cross.

It is sobering how rarely Christians think or speak seriously about the deep corruption of the flesh.

"In me (that is, in my flesh) nothing good lives" (Romans 7:18).

Anyone who truly believes this will cry out, "I see another law in my body, bringing me into captivity to the law of sin... What a miserable person I am! Who will deliver me from this body of death?" (Romans 7:23–24).

Blessed is the person who can go further and say, "I thank God through Jesus Christ our Lord... For the law of the Spirit of life in Christ Jesus has set me free from the law of sin and death" (Romans 7:25; 8:2).

If only we understood God's gracious plan for us: the flesh on the cross, the Spirit in the heart, ruling the whole life.

This spiritual life is not understood enough and not pursued enough. Yet this is exactly what God has promised —and what He will accomplish in anyone who fully surrenders to Him for this purpose.

The Deep Root of Prayerlessness

Here we come to the true root of the problem—the real cause of a prayerless life.

The flesh is capable of saying prayers. It can feel religious for doing so and even quiet the conscience. But the flesh has no desire or strength for the kind of prayer that seeks intimate knowledge of God, rejoices in fellowship with Him, and continually draws on His strength. So the conclusion is unavoidable: the flesh must be denied and put to death.

A Christian who is still living in a carnal state lacks the character and strength needed to pursue God. He is satisfied with prayer out of habit or routine. The glory and blessing of secret prayer remain hidden from him. But eventually, his eyes begin to open. He starts to see that the flesh—with its tendency to pull his heart away from God—is the main enemy that makes powerful prayer impossible.

I once spoke at a conference about prayer, using strong language about the flesh fighting against us and being the cause of our prayerlessness.

Afterward, a minister's wife told me she felt I had spoken too strongly. She admitted she struggled with too little desire for prayer, but she believed her heart was sincerely set on seeking God.

I showed her what Scripture says about the flesh: that everything preventing us from receiving the Spirit is nothing less than the hidden work of the flesh.

Adam was created for fellowship with God and enjoyed that fellowship before the fall. But after the fall, a deep aversion to God immediately entered his nature, and he hid from Him.

This unchanging aversion is the defining mark of the unregenerate human heart. It is the main reason we resist surrendering ourselves to fellowship with God in prayer.

The next day, the minister's wife told me that God had opened her eyes. She confessed that the hostility and unwillingness of the flesh had been the hidden obstacle in her weak prayer life.

So do not look to circumstances to explain the prayerlessness you mourn. Look for the cause where Scripture points to it—in the hidden resistance of the heart toward a holy God.

When a Christian does not fully yield to the Spirit's leading—and this yielding is both God's will and God's work—then that Christian ends up living under the power of the flesh without even realizing it. This life "in the flesh" shows itself in many ways:

- in the quick temper or sudden anger that rises up in you;
- in the lack of love you have often blamed yourself for;
- in the pleasure taken in eating and drinking that your conscience has warned you about;
- in the desire to follow your own will and seek your own honor;
- in the confidence you place in your own wisdom and strength;
- and in your enjoyment of the world—the same enjoyment that leaves you feeling ashamed before God.

All of this is life according to the flesh. "You are still carnal" (1 Corinthians 3:3). Perhaps that verse unsettles you at times. You do not feel full peace and joy in God.

I urge you to take time to answer this question honestly: Have you found here the true cause of your prayerlessness? And do you see how powerless you are to change it?

I live in the Spirit—I have been born again. But I do not walk according to the Spirit. The flesh still rules me. And a carnal life simply cannot pray with spiritual power.

God, forgive me. The carnal life is clearly the cause of my sad and shameful prayerlessness.

THE STORM CENTER ON THE BATTLEFIELD

At the conference, someone mentioned the phrase "strategic position," a term often used when speaking about the great conflict between the kingdom of heaven and the powers of darkness.

When a general chooses where to strike the enemy, he focuses most on the point he considers most critical in the battle.

At the Battle of Waterloo, there was a farmhouse that Wellington immediately recognized as the key position. He refused to spare his troops in holding that ground. The entire victory depended on it. And that is exactly how the battle was won.

It is the same in the conflict between the believer and the powers of darkness. The prayer where we go to spend time alone with God (the "inner chamber") is the place where decisive victory is won.

The enemy uses all his power to lead Christians—especially ministers—to neglect prayer. Satan knows that no matter how excellent the sermon, how inspiring the service, or how faithful the pastoral work, none of it threatens his kingdom if prayer is neglected.

But when the Church shuts herself in with God in the power of the inner chamber—when the soldiers of the Lord receive power from on high while on their knees—then the powers of darkness are shaken, and souls are set free.

In the church, on the mission field, and in the relationship between minister and congregation, everything depends on faithful, powerful prayer.

During the conference, I came across this illustration in

The Christian magazine: Two people are fighting over a certain issue. Let's call them Christian and Apollyon. Apollyon notices that Christian holds a particular weapon that guarantees him victory.

They meet in deadly combat. Apollyon decides that before anything else, he must seize that weapon Christian has and destroy it.

For the moment, the original reason for the fight becomes secondary. The most important question is now this: Who will gain control of the weapon everything depends on? Victory hinges entirely on that.

This is exactly what happens in the conflict between Satan and the believer. The child of God can overcome anything through prayer. So is it any wonder that Satan does everything he can to snatch that weapon away, or at least prevent the Christian from using it?

How does Satan hinder prayer? He tempts us to postpone it or shorten it. He fills our minds with wandering thoughts and endless distractions. He works through unbelief and hopelessness.

Blessed is the prayer warrior who, through all of this, holds firm and continues to use the weapon of prayer. Like our Lord in Gethsemane—the more fiercely the enemy attacked, the more earnestly Jesus prayed. He did not stop until the victory was won.

After listing all the other pieces of spiritual armor, Paul adds: "Pray at all times with all prayer and supplication in the Spirit" (Ephesians 6:18).

Without prayer, the helmet of salvation, the shield of faith, and the sword of the Spirit (the Word of God) have no power. Everything depends on prayer.

God, teach us to believe this and hold onto it.

2
THE FIGHT AGAINST PRAYERLESSNESS

As soon as Christians become convinced of their sin of prayerlessness, their first instinct is to try—often with great determination—to overcome it with God's help.

But sadly, they soon discover how little their efforts achieve. Discouragement sweeps over them, and they begin to think that such a prayer life simply isn't possible for them. They feel they cannot remain faithful.

At prayer conferences over the years, many ministers have openly admitted that it seems impossible for them to maintain such a disciplined life of prayer.

Recently, I received a letter from a minister known for both ability and devotion. He wrote: "For me, it doesn't help to hear more about the life of prayer, about the hard work we must prepare for, or about all the time and effort it will cost. These things discourage me. I've heard them so many times. I've tried repeatedly, and the result has always been disappointment. It does no good to tell me, 'You must pray more, watch yourself more closely, and become a more devoted Christian.'"

My reply was this: "I don't believe that in anything I've spoken or written—whether at the conference or elsewhere—I've emphasized effort or struggle. I am completely convinced that our efforts are useless until we first learn how to abide in Christ through simple faith."

He went on to say: "The message I need is this: 'Make sure your relationship with your living Savior is what it should be. Live in His presence, rejoice in His love, rest in Him.'"

A better message could not be given—if it is rightly understood. "Make sure your relationship with the living Savior is what it should be." This alone is what makes a life of prayer possible.

But we must not comfort ourselves by claiming we have a right relationship with Jesus while the sin of prayerlessness still controls us—while we, along with the whole Church, must admit how weak we are, how unfit we are to pray as we ought: for ourselves, for the Church, and for missions.

But if we recognize that a right relationship with Jesus necessarily includes prayer—both the desire and the power to pray according to God's will—then we finally have something real to rejoice in and rest in.

I share this story to show how easily self-effort leads to discouragement. It blocks all hope of change or victory.

This is the condition of many Christians when they are called to persevere in prayer as intercessors. They feel the task is completely beyond their reach. They believe they lack the strength required for the self-denial and dedication needed for such prayer. They withdraw from it because they imagine it will bring nothing but struggle and unhappiness.

They have tried—in the strength of the flesh—to conquer the flesh. That is impossible.

They have tried to cast out Satan by Satan's power. That can never succeed. Only Jesus can subdue the flesh and the devil.

We have spoken about a kind of struggle that always ends in disappointment and discouragement—the struggle carried out in our own strength.

But there is another kind of struggle that always leads to

victory. Scripture calls it "the good fight of faith" (1 Timothy 6:12)—a fight that begins in faith and is carried out by faith.

We must come to a right understanding of faith and stand firm in it. Jesus Christ is always the author and the finisher of faith.

It's when we come into a right relationship with Him that we can be sure of the help and power He gives.

Just as strongly as we must say first, "Don't try in your own strength. Throw yourself at the feet of Jesus and wait on Him with quiet confidence that He is with you and working in you," we must also say this with equal strength: "Fight in prayer. Let faith fill your heart, and you will be strong in the Lord and in the power of His might."

Here's an illustration that may help:

A committed Christian woman who led a large and effective Bible class once came to her minister deeply troubled.

In her earlier years, she had enjoyed rich blessing in her private time with God—real fellowship with the Lord and His Word. But she had gradually lost that joy. No matter what she tried, she couldn't recover it.

God continued to bless her work, but the joy was gone from her life.

The minister asked what she had done to try to regain the blessing.

"I've tried everything I can think of," she said, "but nothing works."

He then asked her to describe her conversion. She answered quickly and clearly:

"At first I tried everything to improve myself and free myself from sin, but it was useless. Eventually I realized I had to stop trying and simply trust the Lord Jesus to give me His life and His peace. And He did."

"Then why," the minister said, "don't you do the same thing now? When you go to pray, no matter how cold or dark your heart feels, don't try to force yourself into the right attitude. Come before Him honestly and say, 'Lord, You see the state I'm in, and I can't fix it. My only hope is in You.'

"Trust Him—simply and childlike—to have mercy on you, and wait on Him. In that trust, your relationship with Him is right. You bring nothing; He has everything."

Some time later she told him that his advice had helped her. She had learned that faith in the love of Jesus is the only way to enter real fellowship with God in prayer.

Now do you see that there are two kinds of struggle?

The first is when we try to overcome prayerlessness in our own strength. If that is where you are, my advice is simple: "Stop striving on your own. Come helpless to Jesus. He will speak life into your soul."

If you have done this, understand that this is only the starting point. From here, you must become serious and attentive—using your strength and awareness to search your heart and guard against even the smallest drifting away. And above all, overcoming prayerlessness will require surrender to a life of self-sacrifice—the kind of life God truly desires and will bring about in us.

3

HOW TO BE DELIVERED FROM PRAYERLESSNESS AND HOW THIS DELIVERANCE MAY CONTINUE

The biggest thing stopping us from gaining victory over prayerlessness is the secret feeling that we will never actually receive the blessing of being free from prayerlessness.

We've tried to improve before, but nothing has changed. Old habits, the power of the flesh, and the pull of the world around us have all been too strong. So we ask ourselves, What's the point of trying something my heart already tells me is impossible? The change needed in our whole life seems far too great.

If someone asks, "Is such a change really possible?" our tired heart sighs and answers, "Sadly, for me it's completely impossible."

Do you know why we respond like this? It's because we've heard the call to prayer the same way Israel heard the commands of Moses—as a law telling us what to do, but giving us no power to do it.

Moses and the law have never given anyone the ability to obey. Do you honestly long for the courage to believe that freedom from a prayerless life is possible for you, and not just for others? If so, you must learn this great truth: deliverance from prayerlessness is part of the redemption Jesus gives. It is one of the blessings of the New Covenant—something God Himself gives us through Christ.

The Prayer Life

As this becomes clear, the command "Pray without ceasing" (1 Thessalonians 5:17) takes on a new meaning for us.

Hope begins to rise in your heart. The Spirit, who is given to you so that you continually cry out "Abba, Father," will make a real life of prayer possible. Then, instead of feeling discouraged, you will listen with hope to the voice that calls you to repentance.

Many people have gone to their inner chamber overwhelmed with guilt for praying so little. They've promised to change and live differently.

Yet no real blessing came. They didn't have the strength to continue, and their repentance had no lasting power.

Why? Because their eyes were not fixed on the Lord Jesus. If only they had understood, they would have prayed something like this: "Lord, You see how cold and dark my heart is. I know I need to pray, but I feel like I can't. I have no urgency, no desire to pray."

They did not realize that at that very moment, Jesus—full of tender love—was looking at them and saying:

"You can't pray. Everything feels cold and dark. Then put yourself completely in My hands.

"Believe that I am ready to help you pray. I long to pour My love into your heart, so that in your weakness you can rely on Me to give you the gift of prayer.

"Just as I will cleanse you from every other sin, I will free you from the sin of prayerlessness. Only don't look for victory in your own strength.

"Come to Me as someone expecting everything from his Savior. Let your soul be still before Me, no matter how troubled you feel.

"Be confident of this: I will teach you how to pray."

Many Christians eventually realize this and say:

"I see my mistake now. I never thought Jesus had to

deliver me from this sin as well.

"I didn't understand that He was with me every day in my private prayer time—ready in His love to guide and bless me, even when I felt sinful and unworthy.

"I never realized that just as He gives every other kind of gift in answer to prayer, so first and most importantly, He gives the grace of a praying heart.

"How foolish I was to think that every other blessing must come from Him, but that prayer—on which everything else depends—had to be achieved by my own effort!

"Thank God, I'm beginning to understand: Jesus Himself is in the inner room with me.

"He watches over me and takes responsibility for teaching me how to come to the Father. He asks only one thing: that I wait on Him with childlike trust and bring Him glory."

Haven't we all seriously forgotten this truth?

From a weak spiritual life, we can only expect weak prayer. It's pointless for us, with a weak spiritual life, to try to pray more or pray better. We simply can't.

Nothing less is needed than this: we must experience what it means that being in Christ makes us new people. The old has passed away. Everything has become new.

This is literally true for the person who understands and experiences what it means to be in Jesus Christ.

Our whole relationship with Jesus has to become something new.

I must believe in His endless love—a love that really wants fellowship with me at every moment and wants me to enjoy His presence.

I must believe in His power, which has defeated sin and will truly keep me from it.

I must believe in Him as the great intercessor, who

The Prayer Life

through the Spirit gives every member of His body joy and strength for fellowship with God in prayer.

My prayer life needs to come completely under the influence and leadership of Christ and His love. Only then will prayer become what it is meant to be: the natural, joyful breathing of spiritual life.

We breathe in the atmosphere of heaven and breathe it out again in prayer. Do you see that as this faith takes hold of us, the call to a prayer life that pleases God becomes a welcome invitation?

The cry "Turn from the sin of prayerlessness" will no longer bring a sigh of helplessness or resistance from the flesh. We will hear the Father's voice opening the door wide and welcoming us into fellowship with Himself.

Praying for the Spirit's help will no longer feel like too great a burden. It will be simply admitting our weakness at the feet of Jesus and discovering there that victory comes through the strength and love that flow from being with Him.

If the question comes: "Will this continue?" and the fear follows—"You know how many times you've tried before and failed"—then faith will find its confidence not in what you can do, but in the unchanging faithfulness and love of Christ.

He has helped you again and has shown you that those who wait on Him will not be disappointed.

If fear or hesitation still remain, I urge you, in view of God's mercy in Jesus Christ and His unchanging love: throw yourself down at His feet.

Believe with your whole heart that there is real deliverance from the sin of prayerlessness.

"If we confess our sins, He is faithful and just to forgive us our sins and to cleanse us from all unrighteousness" (1 John 1:9).

In His blood and grace there is complete freedom from all unrighteousness—and from all prayerlessness. Praise His name forever!

HOW DELIVERANCE FROM PRAYERLESSNESS MAY CONTINUE

What we've already said about being freed from the sin of prayerlessness also answers another important question: How can this freedom continue?

Redemption is not something God gives us in small amounts or something we only use occasionally. It is a complete, abundant grace stored up for us in the Lord Jesus—grace that becomes real in fresh, daily fellowship with Him.

This truth is so important that it's worth repeating: Nothing can protect you from slipping back into carelessness, and nothing can help you continue in steady, powerful prayer, except daily close fellowship with Jesus.

Jesus said to His disciples: "You believe in God; believe also in Me... Believe Me that I am in the Father and the Father in Me... Whoever believes in Me will do the works I do, and even greater works" (John 14:1, 11–12).

Jesus was teaching His disciples that everything they knew about God's power, holiness, and love from the Old Testament must now be centered on Him. Their faith needed to rest not merely on written words, but on Him personally.

They needed to believe that He was in the Father and the Father was in Him—so fully united that They shared one life and one glory. Everything they saw in Jesus was in God, and everything in God was in Him.

He stressed this because only through this kind of faith in His divine glory could the disciples do the works He did —and even greater ones.

This faith would also teach them that just as Christ and the Father are one, they themselves were in Christ and Christ was in them.

It is this close, personal, ongoing relationship with Jesus that gives power to our lives—especially to our prayer lives.

Let's think about what this really means: all the greatness and character of God are found in Jesus Christ.

1. God's Omnipresence

God fills the world and is present in every place at every moment. And because Jesus shares the same divine nature, He too is present everywhere—especially with each one of His redeemed people.

This is one of the most important truths our faith must learn. We see this clearly in the experience of Jesus' disciples. What was their greatest privilege during His earthly ministry? They enjoyed His presence all the time.

That is why the thought of His death broke their hearts. They feared losing that presence. They believed He would no longer be with them.

So how did Jesus comfort them? He promised that the Holy Spirit would give them an even deeper awareness of His life and personal presence—so real and so constant that He would be closer to them than He had ever been while physically on earth.

This great promise belongs to every believer today, although many Christians experience very little of it.

Jesus Christ—fully divine, and full of the same love that took Him to the cross—wants to be in fellowship with us every moment of the day, and He wants us to enjoy that fellowship.

This is something every new believer should hear clearly: "The Lord loves you so much that He wants you near Him all the time so you can experience His love."

And this is what every struggling believer must learn—especially anyone who feels powerless to pray, obey, or live a holy life. Only this kind of daily closeness with Jesus can give us the strength we need as intercessors—strength to overcome the world and bring souls to Him.

2. God's Omnipotence

How amazing the power of God is! We see it in creation. We see it in the stories of redemption throughout the Old Testament. We see it in the works the Father did through Christ, and above all in His resurrection from the dead.

We are called to believe in the Son just as we believe in the Father. Yes—the Lord Jesus, who in His love is so close to us, is the almighty One for whom nothing is impossible.

Whatever may be in our hearts or in our flesh that refuses to submit, He can and will conquer it.

Everything God has promised in His Word—all that belongs to us as children of the New Covenant—the almighty Jesus is able to give.

When I bow before Him in my private time of prayer, I am connecting with the eternal, unchanging power of God. When I entrust my day to Jesus, I can be sure that His eternal, almighty power covers me and will accomplish everything needed.

If we would simply take the time to be alone with Him so we could fully experience the presence of this almighty Jesus—what blessing we would know through faith! —an Ongoing fellowship with a Lord who is always present and all-powerful.

3. The Holy Love of God

God's holy love means that with His whole heart He offers all that He is—all His divine character and all His power—for our good, and He is ready to give Himself to us.

Christ is the expression of that love. He is the Son given by love, the gift of love, the power of love.

This Jesus, who proved His love beyond all doubt on the cross—through His suffering, bloodshed, and death—comes to meet us in our private time with Him.

He gives us His promise that uninterrupted fellowship with Him is our inheritance, and that through Him it can become our daily experience.

The holy love of God, which gave everything to overcome sin and destroy it, comes to us in Christ to save us from every sin.

Take time to think about Jesus' words: "You believe in God; believe also in Me... Believe that I am in the Father... and that you are in Me, and I am in you" (John 14:1, 11, 20).

This is the secret of a real life of prayer.

Take time in your private place to kneel, worship, and wait on Him—until He makes Himself known to you, takes hold of your heart, and goes out with you to show you how to live in constant fellowship with a Lord you cannot see.

Do you want to know how to continue living free from the sin of prayerlessness? Here is the secret: believe in the Son of God. Give Him time in the inner room to reveal Himself as the One who is always near you—the eternal, almighty Lord, the everlasting love watching over you.

Then you will begin to experience what you may never have known before—human hearts have never fully understood what God is willing to do for those who love Him.

4

THE BLESSING OF VICTORY; THE MORE ABUNDANT LIFE

If we are now being freed from the sin of prayerlessness—and understand how this freedom can continue—what will be the result?

Anyone who sees this clearly will pursue this freedom with fresh determination and perseverance. Their life will show that they have received something of immeasurable value. They will become a living testimony of the blessing that victory brings.

THE BLESSING OF CONSTANT FELLOWSHIP WITH GOD

Think of the confidence in our Father that will take the place of the guilt and self-condemnation that once marked our lives.

Think of the deep awareness that God's power has done something real inside us—something that shows we truly bear His image. We are now fitted for a life of fellowship with Him and ready to bring Him glory.

Think of how we—while still knowing how small and weak we are—may live as true children of a King, walking in fellowship with our Father. We may begin to show something of the character of our Lord Jesus, who lived in constant fellowship with His Father on earth.

Think of how the time spent praying in our private place may become the happiest hour of the day for us.

Think of how God may use us to take part in His purposes and make us sources of blessing to the world around us.

THE POWER WE CAN GET FOR THE WORK WE'RE CALLED TO

The preacher will learn to receive his message directly from God through the power of the Holy Spirit. He will learn to deliver it with that same power to the congregation.

The preacher will discover where he can be filled with love and passion—enough to help him, in his personal visits and pastoral care, meet each person with real compassion.

He will be able to say with Paul: "I can do all things through Christ who gives me strength" (Philippians 4:13). "We are more than conquerors through Him who loved us" (Romans 8:37). "We are ambassadors for Christ... we beg you on Christ's behalf, be reconciled to God" (2 Corinthians 5:20).

These are not empty ideas or wishful thinking. God has given us Paul as an example. Even if we differ from Paul in our gifts or calling, we can still experience what he did—the all-sufficient grace of God that enabled him to do everything he was called to do.

That same grace can work in us exactly as it worked in him.

THE PROSPECT THAT OPENS FOR THE FUTURE

The future that lies before us is a life dedicated to standing as intercessors—carrying the needs of the whole Church and the whole world on our hearts.

Paul urged believers to pray for all the saints. He spoke about the great burden he carried for people who had never even seen him in person.

In his physical body, Paul was limited by time and place. But in the Spirit, he had real power in Christ's name to pray blessing over people who had never heard of the Savior.

Alongside his ordinary life with people on earth—near or far—Paul lived another kind of life: a heavenly life, filled with love and remarkable power in prayer, which he practiced continually.

We can hardly imagine what God would do if we were freed from the sin of prayerlessness and prayed with the boldness that reaches heaven and brings down blessing in the mighty name of Jesus.

What a future that would be! Ministers and missionaries, by God's grace, praying twice as much as before, with twice the faith and twice the joy!

Imagine the difference this would make in preaching, in prayer meetings, and in everyday ministry. Imagine the gentle power that would fill a private place of prayer made holy by closeness with God and His love in Christ.

Think of the influence this would have on believers, urging them toward the work of intercession.

Think of the impact this would have on the Church and among those who do not yet believe.

Think of the effect on ministers in other churches. Who can say how God might use us for His Church worldwide?

Isn't it worth giving up anything necessary and asking God without stopping to give us real and lasting victory over the prayerlessness that has brought us so much loss?

Why do I write these things and speak so highly of victory over "the sin that so easily trips us up" (Hebrews 12:1), the sin that has robbed us of the power God meant us to have?

Here is the reason: I know how small our thoughts often are about God's promises and power. How easily we slip backward. How quickly we limit God. How often we assume it's impossible for Him to do more than we've seen so far.

It is a wonderful thing to discover God in a fresh way in private prayer. But that is only the beginning.

Even greater is discovering God as the One who is completely enough—and waiting on His Spirit to open our hearts and minds wide so we can receive the great things, the new things, He really wants to give to those who wait on Him.

God's purpose is to strengthen our faith and to help His children see that they must take the time to understand and rely on His greatness. Then we can take this promise in a simple, childlike way:

"To Him who is able to do far more than all we ask or imagine... to Him be glory forever" (Ephesians 3:20–21).

If only we understood how great and glorious our God truly is!

Someone may ask, "Could this confidence in certain victory become a danger—leading to pride or carelessness?"

Yes, it could. Anything that is great and good can be misused.

So how do we avoid this? There is no safer way than prayer—real prayer that brings us face-to-face with God.

As we seek God's holiness in consistent prayer, our sinfulness is exposed and humbled.

As we see His greatness, we feel our own smallness.

Closeness with God through Jesus Christ brings us to experience that nothing good comes from ourselves. We can only walk with God as our faith becomes a humble dependence on Him—just as Christ humbled Himself—and as we truly live in Him the way He lives in the Father.

Prayer is not only coming to God to ask for things.

Above everything else, prayer is closeness with God—letting His holiness and His love shape us until He takes hold of our whole being and imprints on us the humility of Christ, which is the foundation of all real worship.

It is only in Christ Jesus that we draw near to the Father—we who have died with Christ and are done with our old life. It is only as people in whom He lives that we can truthfully say, "Christ lives in me" (Galatians 2:20).

Everything said about the work Jesus does to free us from prayerlessness applies not just to the beginning of the prayer life or the joy of discovering new prayer power. It applies to the whole life of prayer—through every hour of the day.

"Through Him we have access to the Father" (Ephesians 2:18). In this—and in every part of spiritual life—Christ is everything. "They saw no one except Jesus" (Matthew 17:8).

May God give us the faith to believe that real victory has been prepared for us, and that the blessing will be greater than anything the human mind has imagined. God will do this for those who love Him.

This does not happen all at once. God is patient with His children. He stays with us in our slow progress, showing the patience of a loving Father.

Let every child of God take joy in everything His Word promises. The stronger our faith becomes, the more steadily we will continue to the end.

THE MORE ABUNDANT LIFE

Jesus spoke about the "more abundant life" when He said He came to give His life for His sheep: "I came that they may have life and have it abundantly" (John 10:10).

A person may have life and still have very little strength

or vitality—because of poor nourishment or illness.

This is the difference between Old Testament life and New Testament life. Under the law there was life, but not the overflowing grace of the New Covenant.

Christ had already given life to His disciples, but they could receive the abundant life only through His resurrection and the coming of the Holy Spirit.

Every true Christian has received life from Christ. But most know nothing about the abundant life He wants to give.

Paul speaks about this constantly. He says about himself that God's grace was "more than abundant" (1 Timothy 1:14).

"I can do all things through Christ who gives me strength" (Philippians 4:13).

"Thanks be to God, who always leads us in triumph in Christ" (2 Corinthians 2:14).

"We are more than conquerors through Him who loved us" (Romans 8:37).

We have spoken about the sin of prayerlessness, how God delivers us from it, and how He keeps us free from it. Everything we've said is included in Jesus' words: "I came that they may have life and have it abundantly."

It is extremely important for us to understand this abundant life, because only then will we see clearly that a true prayer life requires nothing less than living in an ever-increasing experience of that overflowing life.

It is possible to begin the fight against prayerlessness with dependence on Christ—looking to Him for strength—and still end up disappointed.

This happens when we treat prayerlessness as a single, isolated sin we need to battle. In reality, it is part of the entire life of the flesh, connected to many other sins that come from the same source.

We forget that the whole flesh—with all its desires, whether shown in body or mind—must be regarded as crucified and handed over to death.

We should not settle for a weak life. We should seek an abundant life. We must give ourselves fully so the Holy Spirit can take complete possession of us. Then our whole inner life will be changed, and the rule of Christ and the Spirit will be clearly seen.

So what exactly is this abundant life? We cannot say it too often or in too many ways: The abundant life is nothing less than the fullness of Jesus working in every part of our being through the power of the Holy Spirit.

As the Spirit reveals Christ's fullness and the abundant life He gives, three main aspects will become clear:

1. As the Crucified One

Christ is not only the One who died for us to take away our sins. He is also the One who brings us into His death—so that we die with Him. He works the power of His cross and His death inside us.

You have real fellowship with Christ when you can say, "I have been crucified with Christ—He, the crucified One, lives in me" (Galatians 2:20).

The attitudes and character that were in Him—His humility, His obedience, even to the point of death—are what He meant when He said about the Holy Spirit, "He will take what is Mine and show it to you" (John 16:15). Not as ideas, but as actual participation in the same life He lived.

Do you want the Holy Spirit to take full possession of you so that the crucified Christ lives in you? Then understand: this is exactly why the Spirit was given, and He will certainly accomplish it in all who yield themselves to Him.

2. As the Risen One

Scripture often speaks of the resurrection when describing God's supernatural power—the power that raised Christ from the dead. From this comes the assurance of: "the immeasurable greatness of His power toward us who believe, according to the working of His mighty strength, which He exercised in Christ when He raised Him from the dead" (Ephesians 1:19–20).

Don't read over those words quickly. Go back and read them again. Learn this truth: no matter how weak or powerless you feel, God's power is working in you. If you simply believe, this power will give you a share in the risen life of His Son in your daily living.

Yes—through the Holy Spirit, the joy and victory of Christ's resurrection can become the strength of your everyday life, right in the middle of life's trials and temptations.

Let the cross humble you and bring the self-life to an end. God will work His risen, heavenly life in you through His Spirit.

How little we have understood that it is entirely the Spirit's work to make us part of the crucified and risen Christ, and entirely His work to shape us to Christ's life and death.

3. As the Glorified One

The glorified Christ is the One who baptizes with the Holy Spirit. When Jesus was baptized by the Spirit, it was because He had humbled Himself. He joined Himself to a baptism meant for sinners. As He stepped into His work of redemption, He received the Spirit to equip Him for that mission—from that moment until, on the cross, He "offered Himself without blemish to God" (Hebrews 9:14).

Do you want this glorified Christ to baptize you with the Holy Spirit?

Then offer yourself to Him for His work—to take part in making the Father's love known to the world.

May God help us understand how great a thing it is to receive the Holy Spirit with power from the glorified Jesus!

It means having a desire—a longing—to work for Him and, if needed, suffer for Him.

You have known and loved your Lord. You have worked for Him and seen blessing. But the Lord has much more to give.

He can work in us, in the believers around us, and in the ministers of the Church through the Spirit's power in a way that fills our hearts with awe.

Have you embraced this life? The abundant life is nothing less than the full life of Christ—crucified, risen, and glorified—who baptizes with the Holy Spirit and reveals Himself in our hearts as Lord over everything within us.

Recently I read a phrase: "Live in what must be."

Don't live in the small world of what you think is possible. Live in God's Word—in the love and unlimited faithfulness of Jesus.

Even if progress feels slow and includes many stumbles, the faith that keeps thanking Him—not for feelings or experiences, but for His promises—will grow stronger and stronger. It will deepen in the confidence that God Himself will finish His work in us.

5
THE EXAMPLE OF OUR LORD

The connection between the prayer life and the life of the Spirit is close and cannot be separated. We don't only receive the Spirit through prayer—walking in the Spirit requires an ongoing life of prayer.

I can be continually led by the Spirit only as I continually give myself to prayer. We see this clearly in the life of Jesus. Studying His prayer life gives us a powerful picture of prayer's holiness and power.

Think about His baptism. It was while He was being baptized and praying that heaven opened and the Holy Spirit descended on Him.

God wanted to confirm Jesus' surrender—not only to a baptism meant for sinners but to a death meant for sinners—by giving Him the Spirit for the work He had come to do.

But this gift did not come without prayer. In prayerful fellowship with His Father, the Spirit came on Him and led Him into the wilderness for forty days of prayer and fasting.

Now look at Mark 1:32–35: "That evening after sunset, people brought to Him everyone who was sick or demon-possessed... The whole city gathered at the door... Very early in the morning, while it was still dark, He got up, went out to a quiet place, and there He prayed."

The work of that day and evening had exhausted Him. In healing and helping people, strength had gone out from

Him. So while others slept, He withdrew to pray and renew His strength in the Father's presence. He needed this—otherwise He wouldn't have been ready for the next day.

The holy work of helping souls must constantly be renewed by closeness with God.

Consider also the calling of the apostles in Luke 6:12–13: "During those days, He went out to the mountain to pray, and spent the whole night praying to God. When morning came, He called His disciples and chose twelve of them, whom He named apostles."

It's plain that anyone who wants to do God's work must spend time with Him to receive His wisdom and strength.

Recognizing our dependence and weakness opens the door for God to show His power.

How important was the choosing of the apostles—for Jesus' ministry, for the early Church, and for all generations! It carried God's blessing because prayer was behind it.

In Luke 9:18, 20 we read: "While He was praying alone and His disciples were with Him, He asked them, 'Who do the crowds say I am?'... Peter answered, 'God's Messiah.'"

Jesus had prayed that the Father would reveal who He was to His disciples. Peter's confession—"You are the Christ"—was the result of that prayer.

Then in Luke 9:28–35: "He took Peter, John, and James and went up on the mountain to pray. As He was praying, the appearance of His face changed... Then a voice came from the cloud: 'This is My Son, My Chosen One; listen to Him!'"

Jesus wanted the Father to strengthen the disciples' faith with a clear witness from heaven that He was God's Son. Prayer brought this about—for Jesus Himself and for His disciples.

Again we see that whatever God wants to accomplish on

earth depends on prayer. And the way God works through Christ is the same way He works through believers: through hearts open toward heaven in believing prayer.

Now read Luke 11:1–13: "He was praying in a certain place. When He finished, one of His disciples said, 'Lord, teach us to pray…'"

Then He gave them the Lord's Prayer—"Our Father in heaven."

This prayer reveals what was in Jesus' heart when He prayed: that God's name would be honored, His kingdom would come, and His will would be done on earth as it is in heaven. How will this ever happen? Through prayer.

Through the centuries, countless millions have been comforted by this prayer. But never forget this: it was born out of Jesus' own prayer. He had been praying—and therefore could teach them how to pray.

Then in John 14:16: "I will ask the Father, and He will give you another Counselor."

The entire era of the New Testament—the outpouring of the Holy Spirit—came in answer to Jesus' prayer.

It's as if God put this seal on the gift of the Spirit: the Spirit will come in answer to the prayers of Jesus, and in answer to the prayers of His disciples who learn to pray as He did—taking time alone with God and offering themselves fully to Him.

Then there is John 17—the holy "High Priestly Prayer." Here Jesus first prays for Himself, that the Father will glorify Him, give Him strength for the cross, raise Him from the dead, and place Him at His right hand.

These things could only come through prayer.
Prayer had the power to obtain them.

Then He prayed for His disciples: that the Father would keep them from the evil one, protect them from the world, and make them holy.

Then He prayed for everyone who would believe through their message—that all would be one in love, just as the Father and Son are one.

This prayer opens a window into the relationship between the Father and the Son.

It teaches that all the blessings of heaven come through the ongoing prayers of the One who stands at God's right hand and always prays for us.

But it also teaches that we must want these blessings and ask for them in the same spirit.

All the beauty and greatness of God's blessings rests on this: they are given in answer to prayer—when we surrender ourselves to God and believe in the power of prayer.

Finally we come to the most striking example—Gethsemane. Here we see Jesus, as He always did, bringing His work before the Father. First He begged in agony for the cup to pass from Him. When He knew it could not, He prayed for strength to drink it and surrendered Himself completely: "Your will be done."

Because He prayed, He faced the enemy with courage.
In God's strength, He gave Himself to the death of the cross.

Why do God's children have such little confidence in prayer as the great power that bends our wills to God's will, and as the strength to carry out His work in spite of our weakness?

If only we would learn from Jesus how impossible it is to walk with God, receive His guidance, or do His work joyfully and fruitfully without close, ongoing fellowship with Him—the One who is always a living fountain of spiritual life and power!

Let every Christian reflect on this simple study of Jesus' prayer life. Ask God—with the Spirit's help—to teach you from His Word what the life of Jesus is, and what He seeks to live in us.

It is nothing less than a life of daily prayer.

Let every minister especially realize how pointless it is to try to do the Lord's work in any other way than Jesus did it.

Let us, as workers, believe that God sets us apart from much of the world's business so that—above everything else—we may have time. In our Savior's name, with His Spirit, united with Him, we may ask for blessing and receive it—for the world.

6
THE HOLY SPIRIT AND PRAYER

Isn't it sad that when we think about the Holy Spirit, our thoughts are so often mixed with guilt and regret? Yet He is called the Comforter and was given to help us find our deepest joy and delight in Christ.

What's even sadder is this: the One who lives in us to comfort us is often grieved because we won't let Him finish His work of love in us.

The lack of prayer in the Church causes deep sorrow to the Holy Spirit. This same prayerlessness is also the reason for our spiritual weakness and lack of power. It's because we're not willing to let the Holy Spirit lead us.

May God help us think about the Holy Spirit's work in a way that fills us with joy and strengthens our faith.

The Holy Spirit is called "the Spirit of grace and supplication" (Zechariah 12:10). That is His special name.

Twice in Paul's letters we find a striking description of His work in prayer: "You received the Spirit of adoption, by whom we cry, 'Abba, Father'" (Romans 8:15). "God sent the Spirit of His Son into your hearts, crying, 'Abba, Father'" (Galatians 4:6).

Have you ever really thought about these words, "Abba, Father"?

With that name, our Savior prayed His greatest prayer in Gethsemane, giving Himself completely to the Father's will in love and surrender.

The Prayer Life

The Holy Spirit is given so that, from the very beginning of our Christian life, He can teach us to say those same words with childlike trust and willingness to yield.

In one verse it says, "We cry." In the other it says, "He cries." Together they show how God and His children work together in prayer.

This is God's way of showing how far He has gone to make prayer natural and powerful—like a child calling out to a loving father and saying, "Abba, Father."

Isn't it a sign that the Holy Spirit is largely unknown in the Church that prayer—something God has so wonderfully provided for—is often felt as a burden and a duty?

Doesn't this show us that the real root of our prayerlessness lies in our ignorance of the Holy Spirit and in our failure to follow His leading?

If we want to see this even more clearly, we need to look at Romans 8:26–27:

"In the same way, the Spirit helps us in our weakness, because we do not know what to pray for as we should. But the Spirit Himself intercedes for us with sighs too deep for words. And He who searches our hearts knows the Spirit's thoughts, because He intercedes for the saints according to the will of God."

Isn't it clear from this that, left to ourselves, we don't know how to pray or what we should pray for?

God meets us in this weakness by giving us the Holy Spirit Himself to pray for us.

His work goes deeper than our thoughts and feelings, but God sees it and answers it.

So our first concern in prayer should not be to bring many words or ideas to God. Instead, we should come with confidence that the Holy Spirit is already at work in us.

This confidence will quiet our hearts and fill us with reverence. It will help us, as we depend on Him, to lay our needs and desires before God.

The great lesson for every person who prays is this: First of all, place yourself under the Holy Spirit's leading. Rely completely on Him. Give Him the first place. Then your prayer will have a value far beyond what you can imagine. By His help you will learn how to bring your desires to the Father in Jesus' name.

What a safeguard this kind of faith would be against coldness and discouragement in our private prayer time.

Just think of it: in every true prayer, the three Persons of the Godhead are involved. The Father listens. The Son gives us the right to come in His name. The Spirit prays in us and for us.

How important it is, then, that we stand in a right relationship to the Holy Spirit and understand His work.

We need to think seriously about a few things.

1. Let's Firmly Believe, As a Real Fact, That the Holy Spirit Is in Us

Don't assume you already know this and don't need to think about it. This truth is so great that only the Holy Spirit Himself can really write it on our hearts and keep it there.

"The Spirit Himself testifies with our spirit" (Romans 8:16).

Our attitude should be one of steady, confident faith that our hearts are the Holy Spirit's dwelling place—that He lives in us and wants to guide our whole life.

Let's thank God often, especially when we pray, that His Spirit is in us to teach us how to pray. Thanksgiving draws our hearts away from ourselves and toward God. It gives the Spirit room to work in us.

No wonder we've become prayerless and have felt that

prayer is too hard for us—if we've tried to have fellowship with the eternal God on our own, instead of relying on His Spirit, who is given to reveal the Father and the Son to us.

2. As We Practice This Faith — That the Spirit Lives and Works in Us — We Must Also Understand What He Wants to Do in Us

The Holy Spirit's work in prayer is closely connected to everything else He does.

We saw earlier that His first and greatest work is to show us Christ—His constant love and His power. So in prayer, the Holy Spirit will keep directing our attention to Christ, to His blood and His name, which are the solid foundation of our confidence that God hears us.

He is also "the Spirit of holiness," who teaches us to recognize sin, reject it, and leave it behind.

He is "the Spirit of light and wisdom," who leads us into the rich secrets of God's overflowing grace.

He is "the Spirit of love and power," who teaches us how to witness for Christ and work for the good of others with real compassion.

The more closely I connect all these things to the Holy Spirit, the more clearly I will see His divine nature—and the more willing I will be to follow His leading as I seek God in prayer.

What a different life I would have if I truly knew the Holy Spirit as the Spirit of prayer.

There is something else I must continually learn:

3. The Spirit Wants to Have Full Possession of My Life

We often pray for more of the Spirit—and it's right to do so. But we must set that prayer alongside another truth: the Spirit wants more of us.

He wants to take full possession of us. Just as my soul uses my whole body for its home and its service, the Holy Spirit wants my entire being—body and soul—as His dwelling place, fully under His direction.

No one can continue sincerely in prayer without beginning to realize that the Spirit is gently leading them into a new level of surrender they have never known before.

"I seek You with my whole heart" (Psalm 119:10). The Spirit will make words like these more and more the guiding theme of our lives.

He will show us that the double-mindedness still in us is truly sinful. He will reveal Christ as the mighty deliverer from all sin—near at all times to protect and free us.

He will lead us in prayer to forget ourselves, and He will make us willing to be trained as intercessors—people God can trust with His work, who will cry out to Him day and night for His Church and His kingdom.

May God help us to know the Holy Spirit, and to honor Him as the Spirit of prayer!

7

SIN VS. THE HOLINESS OF GOD

To understand grace and Christ correctly, we need to understand what sin really is. We learn this through God's light and His Word.

Come with me to the beginning of the Bible. There we see humanity created by God, made in His image, and declared by Him to be very good.

Then sin entered as rebellion against God. Adam was driven from paradise, and he and countless millions of his descendants came under the curse and ruin that followed. That was the work of sin. Here we see its nature and its power.

Come further and look at Noah's ark resting on Mount Ararat. Human evil had become so terrible that God saw no solution except to wipe humanity from the earth. That was sin's work.

Come again, this time to Mount Sinai. God wanted to form a covenant with the new nation of Israel. But because of human sin, He had to appear in darkness, lightning, and terrifying glory—so overwhelming that Moses said:

"I'm terrified and trembling" (Hebrews 12:21).

And before the giving of the law was finished, this terrible warning came: "Cursed is everyone who does not continue in everything written in the book of the law" (Galatians 3:10). Sin made that necessary.

Now come with me once more—to Calvary. Here we

see what sin really is. Here we see the hatred and hostility of the world casting out and crucifying the Son of God. Here sin reached its highest point.

Here Christ was made sin for us, and became a curse for us, because this was the only way sin could be destroyed.

In the agony of Gethsemane, where He prayed that He would not have to drink the dreadful cup... and in the agony of the cross, where in deep darkness and abandonment He cried out: "My God, My God, why have You forsaken Me?"—here we get at least a faint idea of the curse and indescribable suffering that sin brings.

If anything can teach us to hate and despise sin, it is Christ on the cross.

Come with me again, one last time—to the final judgment. See the bottomless darkness where countless souls will be cast with the sentence: "Depart from Me, you cursed, into the eternal fire" (Matthew 25:41).

Won't these words soften our hearts and leave us with a lasting horror of sin, so we may learn to hate it completely?

Is there anything else that can help us understand what sin is? Yes—look inside yourself and see sin in your own heart. Everything we have seen of sin's ugliness and evil should teach us what sin in our own hearts means.

All the hostility against God... all the ruin it brings to people... all the evil hidden in its nature... all of this lies within the sins we commit and the guilt of every transgression against God.

When you remember that you are a child of God and yet you still sin—sometimes even letting that sin act out its desires—shouldn't you cry out in shame:

"How terrible this is—this sin in me!" "Depart from me, Lord, for I am a sinful person" (Luke 5:8).

One of sin's greatest powers is that it blinds us so we

don't see its true nature. Even Christians excuse themselves by saying they can never be perfect and that sinning every day is unavoidable.

They've become so used to the idea of sinning that they've almost lost the ability to grieve over sin. But there can be no real growth in grace without a growing awareness of the guilt and seriousness of every sin against God.

There's hardly a more important question than this: "How can I regain tenderness of conscience and become able to offer God a truly broken and repentant heart?"

Scripture shows us the way. Let Christians remember how God views sin—how His holiness burns against it, and the great sacrifice He made to defeat it and set us free.

Let us stay in God's presence until His holiness shines into our hearts and we cry out with Isaiah: "I'm ruined!" (Isaiah 6:5).

Let us remember the cross and what Christ's love had to endure there—the unimaginable pain caused by sin.

Let us hear God's voice saying: "Don't do this terrible thing I hate" (Jeremiah 44:4).

Let us take time so the blood and love of the cross can do their full work in us.

Let us see sin for what it really is—not just weakness, but giving our hand to the enemy and acting under his influence.

Isn't this one of the tragic results of our prayerlessness and quick, rushed moments in God's presence—that we've almost lost a true understanding of sin?

Let believers think not only of what redemption cost Christ, but also of the fact that through the Holy Spirit, Christ Himself is offered to them as a gift of extraordinary grace—bringing forgiveness, cleansing, and renewal into their lives.

Let them ask themselves: What response should such love receive? If we would only take time to stay with God long enough to ask these questions, the Holy Spirit would do His work of convicting us of sin. He would give us a completely new view of it.

We would begin to realize that we have truly been redeemed, and that through Christ's power we may live each day sharing in the victory He won over sin on the cross—and show it in the way we live.

What do you think? Do you begin to see that the sin of prayerlessness has had a far more serious effect than you first imagined?

Because our conversations with God have been so rushed and shallow, our sense of sin has become weak. We have very few motives that truly move us to hate sin and run from it.

Nothing—absolutely nothing—except hidden, humble, continual fellowship with God can teach us, as His children, to hate sin the way He wants us to hate it.

Nothing—nothing but the constant nearness and ongoing power of the living Christ—can help us truly see what sin is and detest it as we should.

Without this deeper understanding of sin, we will never think seriously about claiming the victory Christ offers or the victory the Spirit works in us.

O my God, help me see my sin. Teach me to stay in Your presence until Your Spirit lets Your holiness rest on me.

O my God, help me understand my sin—and let that understanding lead me to cling to the promise: "The one who abides in Him does not sin" (1 John 3:6).

Help me to expect this promise to be fulfilled in me.

THE HOLINESS OF GOD

People often say that the Church has lost its sense of sin and of God's holiness.

The inner chamber—our private time with God—is the place where we can learn again to give God's holiness the place it should have in our faith and our daily lives.

If you don't know how to spend half an hour in prayer, take the subject of God's holiness. Bow before Him. Take your time—and give God time—so that He can meet you there. This is serious work, but it brings great blessing.

If you want to grow in staying in God's holy presence, open His Word. Read the book of Leviticus, for example, and notice how God repeatedly commands: "You must be holy, because I am holy." (Leviticus 11:44–45; 19:2; 20:7, 26; 21:8; 22:32)

Even more often, God says: "I am the Lord who makes you holy."

This theme is taken into the New Testament. Peter writes: "Be holy in everything you do, because it is written, 'Be holy, for I am holy'" (1 Peter 1:15–16).

Paul writes: "May He make your hearts blameless in holiness... God did not call us to impurity, but to holiness... The One who calls you is faithful; He will do it." (1 Thessalonians 3:13; 4:7; 5:24)

Only knowing God as the Holy One can make us holy. And how will we come to know Him like this except in the private prayer space with God§?

It is impossible unless we take time for it and allow God's holiness to shine on us.

How can anyone come to really know a wise and remarkable person without spending time with them and placing themselves under their influence?

In the same way, how can God sanctify us unless we

take time to experience the power of His holy presence?

Nowhere else can we learn God's holiness or come under its influence except when alone with God. It has been well said: "No one can expect to grow in holiness who is not often, and for long periods, alone with God."

What Is the Holiness of God?

The holiness of God is the highest, most glorious, and most all-encompassing of all His attributes. "Holiness" is one of the deepest words in Scripture—truly a word that belongs to heaven.

Both Testaments affirm this. Isaiah heard the seraphim, with their faces covered, crying: "Holy, holy, holy is the Lord of hosts." (Isaiah 6:3)

John heard the living creatures say: "Holy, holy, holy, Lord God Almighty." (Revelation 4:8)

This is the highest expression of God's glory in heaven—spoken by beings who live in His immediate presence and fall down before Him.

Can we really imagine that simply thinking, reading, or hearing about holiness will help us understand it or become partakers of it? Of course not.

Oh, may we begin to thank God that He has given us the inner chamber—a place where we can be alone with Him and take time to pray:

"Lord, let Your holiness shine more and more into my heart, so that I may become holy."

Let our hearts feel real shame over our prayerlessness, which has made it impossible for God to share more of His holiness with us.

Let us earnestly ask God to forgive this sin, to draw us by His grace, and to strengthen us so we can stay in fellowship with Him—the Holy God.

I've said the meaning of "the holiness of God" cannot

be captured easily in words. But we can begin by saying this: God's holiness is His complete and absolute hatred of sin. If you want to understand that, remember that He chose to see His own Son die rather than allow sin to rule.

Think of God's Son, who gave up His life rather than act—even once—against His Father's will.

Even more, Christ hated sin so deeply that He would rather die than leave the human race under its power.

That is part of God's holiness, and it is His guarantee that He will do everything needed to free us from sin.

God's holiness is like a fire—it consumes sin in us and makes us holy offerings, pure and pleasing to Him.

This is why the Spirit came as fire. He is the Spirit of God's holiness—the One who makes us holy.

So spend time thinking about God's holiness. Bow before Him until you are filled with confidence that the Holy One will work in you.

Take a week if necessary—reading and rereading what Scripture says about God's holiness—until your heart feels the weight of this truth:

"This is the glory of the inner chamber—to meet with the Holy God, to bow in humility and shame because our prayerlessness has dishonored Him and His love." There we will find the assurance that He will welcome us again into fellowship with Himself.

No one should expect to understand or receive God's holiness unless they are often—and for long periods—alone with Him.

Someone has said that God's holiness expresses two things at once: the indescribable distance between God and us because of His righteousness, and the indescribable nearness He desires because of His love.

Bow in humble reverence as you think about the immeasurable distance between you and God. Bow with childlike confidence as you think about His longing to draw you into deep, intimate fellowship with Himself.

Trust completely that He will reveal His holiness to every soul that thirsts for Him, waits on Him, and becomes quiet before Him.

See how the two sides of God's holiness meet at the cross. God's hatred of sin was so great that when sin was placed on Christ, God had to hide His face from Him, leaving Him in terrible darkness.

Yet God's love was so deep, and His desire to unite us with Himself so strong, that He didn't spare His Son but gave Him over to indescribable suffering—so that He could welcome us, in Christ, into His holiness and hold us close as His beloved children.

Jesus spoke of this when He said: "I sanctify Myself for their sakes, so they also may be sanctified by the truth." (John 17:19) Because of this, Christ became our sanctification—and in Him we are made holy.

I beg you—don't underestimate the grace of having a Holy God who longs to make you holy. Don't overlook His call inviting you to give Him time in the quiet of the inner chamber so He can let His holiness rest on you.

Make it your daily work, in the secret place, to meet with the Holy God. You will find that every sacrifice of time or effort is more than rewarded.

You will learn to hate sin—to see it as defeated and detestable. Your new nature will begin to recoil from sin.
The living Jesus, the Holy God, will become your strength—your victory. You will begin to believe the great promise of 1 Thessalonians 5:23–24:

"May the God of peace Himself make you completely holy... The One who calls you is faithful, and He will do it."

8
OBEDIENCE AND THE VICTORIOUS LIFE

The opposite to sin is obedience. "For just as through one man's disobedience many were made sinners, so also through one Man's obedience many will be made righteous… You became slaves of righteousness." (Romans 5:19; 6:18)

As we think about sin, the new life, and receiving the Holy Spirit, we must give obedience the place God gives it. It was because Christ humbled Himself and became obedient to the point of death—even death on a cross—that God highly exalted Him. And Paul, referring to this, urges us: "Let this mind be in you which was also in Christ Jesus." (Philippians 2:5)

More than anything else, we see that Christ's obedience—so pleasing to the Father—must become the defining attitude and pattern of our lives.

Just as a servant knows he must obey his master in everything, so surrender to complete, unquestioning obedience must become the essential quality of our walk with God.

But how little Christians understand this. How many people have convinced themselves that sin is unavoidable—that "everyone sins every day"—and they become content with this idea.

It is impossible to measure the harm this mistake has caused. It's one of the main reasons why the sin of disobedience is barely recognized.

I've heard Christians talk about their failures—about darkness and weakness—and say half-jokingly, "Yes, it's just disobedience again."

If we had a servant who was disobedient every day, we'd get rid of them immediately. But it's treated as nothing unusual when a child of God lives in daily disobedience.

Disobedience is acknowledged every day, yet there's no turning away from it.

Isn't this exactly why so many prayers for the Holy Spirit's power seem to go unanswered?

Acts 5:32 tells us that God gives His Spirit to those who obey Him.

Every believer has received the Holy Spirit. If they use the measure they've been given with the sincere intent to obey God fully, then God can—and will—give them more of the Spirit's power.

But if they allow disobedience to rule their lives day after day, they shouldn't be surprised if their prayers for "more of the Spirit" remain unanswered.

We've already said that the Spirit wants more of us. How can we surrender ourselves fully to Him unless we obey Him?

Scripture tells us we must be led by the Spirit and walk by the Spirit. Our relationship with the Holy Spirit is only right when we let Him guide and direct us.

Obedience is the central issue in our relationship with God. "Obey My voice, and I will be your God." (Jeremiah 7:23; 11:4)

Look at Jesus' words on the night before His death, when He gave His great promise about the Holy Spirit.

"If you love Me, keep My commands. And I will ask the Father, and He will give you another Counselor." (John 14:15–16)

Obedience was essential preparation for receiving the

Spirit. Jesus repeated this truth often: "The one who has My commands and keeps them is the one who loves Me. And the one who loves Me will be loved by My Father, and I will love him and reveal Myself to him." (John 14:21)

Also in verse 23 we read: "If anyone loves Me, he will keep My word. My Father will love him, and We will come to him and make Our home with him."

"If you remain in Me and My words remain in you, ask whatever you wish, and it will be done for you" (John 15:7).

"If you keep My commands, you will remain in My love" (verse 10).

"You are My friends if you do what I command you" (verse 14).

Could anything make it clearer that life in the new covenant—the life made possible after Christ's resurrection—depends on obedience?

This is the Spirit of Christ. He lived not to do His own will, but the Father's. He cannot make His home in the heart of someone who refuses to fully surrender to a life of obedience.

Yet how few Christians take their disobedience seriously. How few believe that Christ really expects obedience from us—because He Himself has taken responsibility to make it possible.

How often is obedience reflected in our prayers, our daily walk, or the hidden places of the soul?
How often do we sincerely try to please the Lord in everything?

We speak far too lightly about our disobedience. "I will be sorry for my sin" (Psalm 38:18) is said—but rarely followed with real repentance.

But is obedience actually possible? Yes—absolutely—for the person who believes Jesus Christ is their sanctification and depends on Him.

Just as someone whose eyes have not yet been opened cannot understand that Christ can instantly forgive sin, many do not yet see that Christ also gives real power to do what God commands.

The same faith that brought us forgiveness now brings deliverance from the power of the sin that has entangled us. By trusting Christ in a new way, we receive His keeping power as something real and constant in our lives.

This faith opens our eyes to promises we once passed over: "Now may the God of peace... equip you with everything good for doing His will, working in us what is pleasing in His sight, through Jesus Christ" (Hebrews 13:20–21).

"Now to Him who is able to protect you from stumbling... be glory and majesty" (Jude 24–25).

"Make every effort to confirm your calling and election... for if you do these things, you will never stumble" (2 Peter 1:10).

"So that He may establish your hearts blameless in holiness" (1 Thessalonians 3:13).

"But the Lord is faithful; He will strengthen and guard you from the evil one" (2 Thessalonians 3:3).

When the soul realizes that the fulfillment of these promises is secured in Christ—that they are as sure as the promise of forgiveness—then, for the first time, obedience is understood correctly.

Faith can rest confidently on a complete Christ and His continual protection.

This faith gives obedience a completely new meaning. Christ Himself takes responsibility to work obedience in me at every moment—if I rely on Him. Then I begin to understand the phrase Paul uses at the start and end of Romans: "the obedience of faith." (Romans 1:5; 16:26)

Faith brings me to Jesus not only for forgiveness, but also

so that His power can help me live as God's obedient child every moment.

Scripture says that as He who called us is holy, so we also must be holy in everything we do.

Everything depends on whether I trust the whole Christ—with all the fullness of His grace—to be my strength every moment, not just occasionally.

Such faith leads to obedience that enables me to "walk worthy of the Lord, fully pleasing to Him, bearing fruit in every good work... strengthened with all power according to His glorious might" (Colossians 1:10–11).

A soul nourished by such promises will no longer struggle toward obedience in its own strength.
Instead, it will experience the obedience of faith—the obedience that flows from Christ living and working within.

All these promises have their certainty and power in the living Christ.

The Victorious Life

Earlier, in the chapter on "The More Abundant Life," we looked mainly at Christ's side of things. We saw that in Him—the crucified, risen, and glorified Lord who baptizes with the Holy Spirit—we find everything needed for a life overflowing with grace.

Now, in speaking of the victorious life, we look at the subject from another angle: How can a Christian truly live as a conqueror?

We've said many times that the prayer life cannot be improved by treating prayer alone. It is inseparably tied to the whole spiritual life. Only when the entire life—which once lacked prayer—is renewed and made holy can prayer take its true place of power.

We must not settle for anything less than the victorious life God calls His children to.

You remember the seven letters in Revelation. Each ends with a promise "to the one who overcomes."

Take time to read those seven promises again. Notice how glorious they are. And they were given even to churches like: Ephesus, which had lost its first love, Sardis, which had a reputation for life but was spiritually dead, Laodicea, which was lukewarm and self-satisfied. This shows that if they would repent, they could still win the crown.

The call to overcome comes to every Christian. It is impossible to be a healthy Christian—and even more impossible to be a minister with real spiritual power—unless everything is surrendered for the sake of victory.

But how do we attain victory? The answer is simple: Everything is in Christ. "Thanks be to God, who always leads us in triumph in Christ." (2 Corinthians 2:14)

"In all these things we are more than conquerors through Him who loved us." (Romans 8:37)

Everything depends on our relationship with Christ—complete surrender, confident faith, and unbroken fellowship with Him.

You want to know how to enter this life? Here are the simple steps to receiving what Christ has prepared for you:

A new discovery of sin.

A new surrender to Christ.

A new faith in His power to help you persevere.

1. A NEW DISCOVERY OF SIN

In Romans 3 we find the understanding of sin that is necessary in repentance for forgiveness: "so that every mouth may be shut, and the whole world may become subject to God's judgment" (Romans 3:19).

At conversion, that's where you took your stand. You

recognized your sin—whether clearly or only dimly—confessed it, and received mercy.

But if you want to live the victorious life, something more is needed. This comes when you learn, through real experience, that in you—that is, in your flesh—"nothing good lives" (Romans 7:18).

You rejoice in God's law in your inner being, yet you see another power at work in your body, pulling you into captivity under the law of sin. It forces you to cry out: "What a wretched person I am! Who will rescue me from this body of death?" (Romans 7:24)

This goes much deeper than your first repentance. At conversion you thought mainly about individual sins—many or few. But now you discover something far more serious:

As a Christian, you still have no power in yourself to do the good you want to do.

You must come to a new and deeper understanding of the sinfulness in your nature, and your complete inability—even as a believer—to live the way you should by your own strength. And so you learn to cry out: "Who will rescue me? I am helpless—a prisoner under sin's power!"

The answer is: "I thank God through Jesus Christ our Lord." (Romans 7:25)

Then Romans 8 opens a new revelation of what you have in Christ. It goes beyond the forgiveness described in Romans 3. You discover that you are in Christ Jesus, and that: "the law of the Spirit of life in Christ Jesus has set you free from the law of sin and death" (Romans 8:2)

Under that old law, you were bound and defeated. Now the Spirit's power has freed you. And that freedom calls you, with a new depth of surrender, to acknowledge Christ as the One who gives victory.

2. A New Surrender to Christ

You may have used the words surrender or consecration many times—but without truly understanding them.

When the message of Romans 7 finally brings you to see how hopeless it is to live a real Christian life—or a real prayer life—by your own effort, you begin to see something clearly:

Only the Lord Jesus, by His own power, can take you up and hold you. He must take possession of you by His Spirit in a new way and in a deeper measure.

Only His power can keep you from falling back into sin again and again. Only His indwelling life can make you victorious.

This realization turns your eyes away from yourself. You become free from self-confidence, and you begin to expect everything from Jesus.

When this dawns on you, you are ready to admit something you once resisted: Nothing good lives in your old nature. It is under the curse. It was nailed to Christ's cross.

You begin to understand Paul when he says we died to sin through Christ's death. And because of that, we now share in His resurrection life.

With this insight, you are encouraged to believe that Christ—through His life in you and His continual presence—can keep you completely.

Just as you had no rest at conversion until you knew He had received you, so now you feel the need to come to Him again—to receive the assurance that He has taken it upon Himself to keep you by the power of His risen life.

You sense that this requires a definite act on your part, just as real as the act by which you first came to Him for forgiveness.

And even though it feels too big, too much to expect, the person who throws themselves without reserve into Christ's arms will discover that He truly receives them
and brings them into fellowship where, from the very beginning onward, they become "more than conquerors."

3. A New Faith in the Power That Will Make It Possible for You to Persevere in Your Surrender

You've heard of Keswick and the truth it emphasizes: Christ is ready to take full responsibility for the daily care and preservation of your life—every day, all day long—if you trust Him to do it.

In many testimonies from believers, this one point stands out again and again. People have shared how they felt called to a deeper surrender—to give every part of their lives to Christ, even the smallest details.

But something held them back: the fear of failure.

Their longing for holiness, for unbroken fellowship with Jesus, for a life of steady, childlike obedience pulled them forward. But a question kept rising up: "Will I stay faithful?"

There was no answer—until they realized this: The surrender Christ asks for cannot be made in our own strength. Christ Himself must give us the power to surrender. He not only keeps us in the future—He first enables us to entrust that future to Him.

It is in Christ's own power that a believer is able to present themselves fully to Him.

Christian, believe this: There is such a thing as a victorious life. Christ the Victor is your Lord. He Himself will take responsibility for you in everything and will enable you to do all that the Father asks.

Take courage.

Will you not trust Him to do this work for you—He who gave His life for you and has forgiven your sins?

Dare, by His strength, to surrender yourself to the life of a person kept from sin by God's power.
Alongside the deepest conviction that nothing good lives in you, confess this truth:

In Jesus, you have everything you need for the life of a child of God. Begin to live literally "by faith in the Son of God, who loved me and gave Himself for me" (Galatians 2:20).

BISHOP MOULE'S TESTIMONY

Let me encourage you with the testimony of Bishop Handley Moule—a man of deep humility and sincere devotion.

When he first heard about Keswick, he feared it taught "perfectionism" and wanted nothing to do with it. But during a quiet vacation in Scotland, he unexpectedly attended a small gathering with some friends. There he heard a message that convinced him the teaching was entirely scriptural.

There was no claim of sinlessness in the flesh, or human perfection. It was simply the truth that Jesus can keep a sinful person from sinning as they trust Him. Light broke into his heart. This man—already regarded as a tender and devoted Christian—found himself stepping into a new experience of what Christ is willing to do for anyone who gives themselves fully to Him.

Here is what Bishop Moule wrote about Philippians 4:13, "I can do all things through Christ who strengthens me": "I dare to say that it's possible for anyone who truly counts on the Lord's power—for keeping and for victory—to live a life where His promises are taken exactly as they are written, and are found to be true.

It's possible to cast all our care on Him day by day, and enjoy deep peace in doing so.

It's possible to have the thoughts and imaginations of our hearts purified, in the fullest meaning of the word, through faith.

It's possible to see God's will in everything and to receive it not with sighing, but with singing.

It's possible, in the hidden life of desire and feeling, to lay aside bitterness, anger, and unkind speech—not occasionally, but every day and every hour.

It's possible, by taking complete refuge in divine power, to become strong through and through. Where our greatest weakness once was, to find now that the very things which used to overthrow our resolve—to be patient, or pure, or humble—become opportunities, through Him who loved us and works in us, for a blessed sense of His presence and His power to make sin powerless.

These things are divine possibilities. Because they are His work, the true experience of them will always bring us lower at His feet, thirsty for more.

We cannot be satisfied with anything less than—each day, each hour, each moment, in Christ, by the Spirit's power—walking with God."

Thank God that a life of victory is certain for those who see their inward ruin and refuse to rely on themselves. But who, in what Moule called "the confidence of despair," look to Jesus alone—and, trusting His power to enable their surrender, actually make that surrender in His strength.

And now, having entrusted everything to Him, they rely on Him alone every day and every hour.

9
HINTS FOR THE INNER CHAMBER

At the conference, a brother who had honestly confessed his neglect of prayer—but later testified that his eyes had been opened to see that the Lord truly gives grace for everything He asks of us—requested some practical guidance. He asked if we could offer a few simple hints on how to spend time well in the inner chamber.

There was no opportunity then to answer. Perhaps the following thoughts will help:

1. **When You Enter the Inner Chamber, Begin by Thanking God**

Thank Him for His incredible love—love that actually invites you to come to Him and speak with Him freely.

If your heart feels cold, dull, or unresponsive, remember: faith does not begin with emotion. It begins with a decision of the will.

Lift your heart to God and thank Him for the fact—not the feeling—that He sees you, welcomes you, and is ready to bless you.

This simple act of faith honors God and gently turns your attention away from yourself.

Think of the grace of Jesus, who is ready to teach you to pray and willing to give you the desire to pray.

Think also of the Holy Spirit, given specifically to cry "Abba, Father" within you and to help you in your weakness.

Spend even five quiet minutes this way, and you will find your faith strengthened for everything that follows in the inner chamber.

So again: start with thanksgiving. Thank God for the privilege of the inner chamber and for His promised blessing there.

2. Prepare Your Heart for Prayer Through Prayerful Bible Reading

One of the biggest reasons people struggle in the inner chamber is this: They don't actually know how to pray. They begin with a few words, run out quickly, and don't know what else to say. They forget that prayer is not a monologue but a conversation. God speaks through His word; we answer Him, respond to Him, and then bring our requests.

So read a few verses. Don't get bogged down in difficulties—save those for another time. Take what you do understand, apply it to yourself, and ask the Father to make that word alive and powerful in your heart.

This will give you plenty to pray about, because you'll be responding to what God is already saying to you. And from there, you'll find freedom to ask for what you truly need.

Keep going in this way, and the inner chamber will no longer feel like a place of sighing and effort. It will become a place of living fellowship with your Father in heaven.

Prayerful Bible meditation is essential for meaningful prayer.

3. After Receiving God's Word, Move Into Prayer—Slowly and Reverently

Don't rush.
Don't assume you already know how to pray.
Prayer offered in your own strength brings little blessing.
Take a moment to quiet yourself before God. Remember who He is—His greatness, His holiness, His love.
Think intentionally about what you want to bring to Him.
Don't settle for repeating the same words every day. A child doesn't say the same sentence to their father day after day. Real conversation reflects the real needs of the moment.
Let your prayer be specific—flowing out of either: the Scripture you just read, or the real needs of your heart that you long to see met.
Let your prayer be clear enough that when you leave the inner chamber you can honestly say, "I know what I've asked my Father for—and I'm expecting an answer."
Sometimes it helps to take a sheet of paper and write down what you want to pray about. Keep that list for a week or more, repeating those prayers until new needs arise.

4. Everything Said So Far Applies to Your Own Needs

But remember—you're also invited to pray for the needs of others.
One of the big reasons inner-chamber prayer often lacks joy and power is that it's too focused on ourselves. Self-centered prayer kills prayer.
Think of your family.

The Prayer Life

Think of your church and its needs.
Think of your neighborhood.
Think of missions and the work of the global church.
Let your heart stretch wide. Become an intercessor.
You'll discover a kind of blessing in prayer you've never experienced before—because God will actually use your prayers to bring blessing into the lives of others.

You'll realize you truly have something to say to God, and you'll begin to see Him do things in answer to your prayers that would not have happened otherwise.

A small child asks their father for bread. A grown child talks with their father about his business and plans. In the same way, an immature Christian prays mostly for themselves.

A more mature Christian learns how to pray with God about the concerns of His kingdom.

Include on your prayer list the names of those you intercede for—your pastor, other spiritual leaders, mission fields you support.

Then the inner chamber will truly become a place where you taste God's goodness—a deep well of joy. It will become the most blessed place in your life.

It may sound like an exaggeration, but it is simply true: God will turn your inner chamber into a Bethel—a place where heaven touches earth—and you will say, "The Lord will be my God." He will also make it a Peniel—a place where you meet God face-to-face and wrestle through to victory.

5. Don't Forget the Connection Between the Inner Chamber and the Outer World

The posture of the inner chamber must carry into the day. Its purpose is to anchor us to God so we walk with Him continually.

Sin, carelessness, and giving in to the flesh or the world will disrupt that fellowship and dim the soul.

If you stumble, go straight back to the inner chamber. Your first act should be to call on the blood of Jesus and claim His cleansing.

Don't rest until—through confession and repentance—you've put away your sin. Let the blood of Christ restore your freedom and confidence before God.

And remember: the roots of your inner-chamber life should extend into everything—your work, your conversations, your decisions.

Let the obedience of faith, which shapes your hidden life, also shape the visible one.

The inner chamber is meant to bind you to God, to fill you with His strength, and to empower you to live for Him alone.

Thank God for the inner chamber—and for the blessed life He'll nurture in you there.

TIME

Before God created the world, time didn't exist. God lived in eternity in a way we can hardly understand.

When creation began, time began—and everything He made was placed under its flow. God set a law over all living things: growth takes time.

Think about it: A child takes years to develop into an adult in body, mind, and maturity. Learning any skill—wisdom, business, craftsmanship, leadership—requires patience and consistency. Everything meaningful takes time. It's exactly the same in the spiritual life.

There can be no real conversation with a holy God, no deep fellowship between heaven and earth, and no power to help save or restore others unless we set aside real time to be with Him.

The Prayer Life

Just as a child must eat and learn every day for many years, so the life of grace depends entirely on the time we're willing to give it, day after day.

A minister is called by God to help people with ordinary jobs see this truth and use their time wisely to preserve and grow their spiritual life.

But a minister cannot do that unless they themselves truly live a life of prayer. Their highest calling isn't preaching, teaching, or pastoral visiting—it's cultivating the life of God in their own soul and becoming a witness of what the Lord is teaching them and doing in them.

Wasn't this true of Jesus? Why did He—who had no sin to confess—choose to spend whole nights in prayer?

Because the divine life in Him was continually strengthened through fellowship with His Father. And through His own life of making time for God, He opened that same life to us.

Oh, that every minister would understand: the time God has given you carries a sacred responsibility. God must receive the first and best part of it for fellowship with Him.

Without this, your preaching and all your work will have little real power.

Here on earth, I can spend my time in exchange for money, knowledge, or accomplishments.

But a minister can exchange their time for divine power —for spiritual blessing poured down from heaven.

That alone makes someone a true servant of God.

That alone brings preaching that has the demonstration of the Spirit and power.

10
THE EXAMPLE OF PAUL

"Be imitators of me, as I also am of Christ."
(1 Corinthians 11:1)

1. PAUL WAS A MINISTER WHO PRAYED CONSTANTLY FOR HIS CONGREGATION

Let's read Paul's words slowly and prayerfully so we can hear the Spirit speaking through them.

"Night and day we pray earnestly... that we might supply what is lacking in your faith... May the Lord make you increase... so that He may establish your hearts blameless in holiness." (1 Thessalonians 3:10–13)

"May the God of peace Himself sanctify you completely." (1 Thessalonians 5:23)

What rich material for meditation!

"Now may our Lord Jesus Christ Himself... comfort your hearts and strengthen you in every good work and word." (2 Thessalonians 2:16–17)

"I mention you constantly in my prayers... that I may impart some spiritual gift to strengthen you." (Romans 1:9–11)

"My heart's desire and prayer to God for them is that they may be saved." (Romans 10:1)

"I never stop giving thanks for you, remembering you in my prayers. I pray that the God... may give you a spirit of wisdom and revelation in knowing Him... so you may understand... the immeasurable greatness of His power toward us who believe." (Ephesians 1:16-19)

"For this reason I kneel before the Father... that He may strengthen you with power through His Spirit in your inner being, so that Christ may live in your hearts through faith... that you may be filled with all the fullness of God." (Ephesians 3:14-19)

"In all my prayers for you, I always pray with joy... I pray that your love will keep growing... so you may be filled with the fruit of righteousness." (Philippians 1:4, 9-11)

"And my God will supply all your needs according to His riches in glory in Christ Jesus." (Philippians 4:19)

"We haven't stopped praying for you... asking that you be filled with the knowledge of His will... so you may walk worthy of the Lord... being strengthened with all power according to His glorious might." (Colossians 1:9-11)

"I want you to know how much I'm struggling for you... and for all who haven't seen me personally. I want their hearts to be encouraged and united in love." (Colossians 2:1-2) What a powerful study for the inner chamber.

These passages show that unceasing prayer was a major part of Paul's ministry. We see the high spiritual goals he aimed at in caring for God's people. We see the tender, self-giving love that led him to keep remembering the churches and their needs before God.

May God bring each of us—and all who minister His word—into the kind of life where prayer like this naturally flows out of us.

We'll have to return to these Scriptures again and again if we truly want the Spirit to lead us into the apostolic life God has set before us as our example.

2. PAUL WAS A MINISTER WHO ASKED HIS CONGREGATION TO PRAY CONSTANTLY

Read these words again with prayerful attention:

"I urge you, brothers and sisters, by our Lord Jesus Christ and by the love of the Spirit, to join me in earnest prayer to God for me. Pray that I may be rescued from the unbelievers in Judea." (Romans 15:30–31)

"We have placed our hope in God... He will continue to rescue us. And you can join in helping through your prayers for us." (2 Corinthians 1:9–11)

"Pray at all times in the Spirit with every kind of prayer and request. Stay alert with all perseverance and intercession for all the saints, and also for me—that words may be given to me when I open my mouth, so I can boldly make known the mystery of the gospel... Pray that I may speak as boldly as I should." (Ephesians 6:18–20)

"I know that this will lead to my deliverance through your prayers and the help of the Spirit of Jesus Christ." (Philippians 1:19)

"Devote yourselves to prayer; stay alert in it with thanksgiving. Pray also for us, that God may open a door for the message... so I can make it clear, as I should." (Colossians 4:2–4)

"Finally, brothers and sisters, pray for us—that the word of the Lord may spread rapidly and be honored." (2 Thessalonians 3:1)

Paul had a deep understanding of the unity of Christ's body and the way believers depend on one another. When the Holy Spirit works strongly in us, He opens our eyes to the same truth.

Paul also shows us something else: he had full confidence that in Rome, Corinth, Ephesus, Colossae, Philippi, and everywhere else, there were believers who would pray with real power—prayers that would reach heaven and move the heart of God.

What a lesson for every minister.

The Prayer Life

Do we truly value the unity of the body of Christ?

Are we trying to raise up believers who know how to intercede? Do we understand that Paul could ask boldly for prayer because he himself prayed powerfully for the churches?

Let's learn from him and ask God to help ministers and congregations grow together in the grace of prayer—so that their entire ministry and life will show that the Spirit of prayer is truly at work among them.

Then we can be confident that God will act for His elect who cry out to Him day and night.

MINISTERS OF THE SPIRIT

What does Scripture mean when it says a minister of the gospel is a "minister of the Spirit"? (2 Corinthians 3:6, 8)

It means this: A preacher must be entirely under the Spirit's direction and power, available for the Spirit to use however He chooses.

Many people pray for the Spirit so they can use Him for their work. That's completely backward. The Spirit must use you. Your posture toward Him must be one of deep dependence and full surrender. He must have you—completely, constantly, in everything.

Some think that if they simply preach the Word, the Spirit will make it effective. They don't realize the deeper truth: the Spirit works through the preacher. The Spirit in the preacher brings the Word to life in the listener's heart.

So it's not enough to pray, "Lord, bless the words I preach." The Lord wants His ministers to be filled with the Spirit, so they speak in the Spirit's life and power.

We see this clearly at Pentecost. They were filled with the Spirit; then they began to speak—and they spoke with power because the Spirit was working in them.

This is the relationship God wants every minister to have with the Spirit. A minister must be convinced: The Spirit lives in them.

The Spirit teaches them and strengthens them day by day. The Spirit empowers their preaching, their conversations, and their pastoral work. Nothing in ministry can be done fruitfully without the Spirit's help. Ministers must live in continual prayer so they can be kept and strengthened by His power.

When Jesus promised the apostles that they would receive power when the Holy Spirit came on them, and commanded them to wait for Him, He was essentially saying:

"Don't attempt to preach until you have this power. This is the foundational preparation for your ministry. Everything depends on it."

So what should we learn from the phrase "ministers of the Spirit"?

Sadly, very little of this seems to be understood or practiced. Few live this way. Few experience the Spirit's power flowing through their ministry.

What must we do? We need a deep confession of guilt —that we have repeatedly grieved the Spirit by not living as His ministers.

We need a simple, childlike surrender to His leading, trusting completely that the Lord will change us.

And we need daily fellowship with Jesus in unbroken prayer, because He alone gives the Holy Spirit as rivers of living water.

11

THE WORD AND PRAYER; PREACHING AND PRAYER; WHOLEHEARTEDNESS

A little of the Word with little prayer leads to spiritual death.

A lot of the Word with little prayer leads to a weak, unhealthy spiritual life.

Much prayer with little of the Word gives more life, but without steadiness.

A full measure of both the Word and prayer every day leads to a strong, healthy, powerful spiritual life.

Think of Jesus. From His youth into adulthood, He treasured God's Word. In the wilderness, in every confrontation with evil, and even in His final cry from the cross—"My God, My God, why have You forsaken Me?"—His heart was filled with Scripture.

And in His prayer life He showed two great truths: The Word gives us material for prayer and encourages us to expect everything from God.

Only through prayer can we live in such a way that every word of God is fulfilled in us.

How do we reach this kind of life, where both the Word and prayer have their full place in us?

There's only one way: our whole life must be transformed. We need a new, healthy, heavenly way of living, where hunger for God's Word and thirst for God naturally express themselves in prayer—just as physical needs naturally make us eat or drink.

Every sign of the flesh's power in us, and every sign of weakness in our spiritual life, should convince us that only the Holy Spirit's living power can create this kind of inner life.

Oh, if only we understood that the Holy Spirit is both the Spirit of the Word and the Spirit of prayer! He will make the Word a joy and a light in our hearts, and He will just as surely help us in prayer—showing us God's will and teaching us to delight in it.

If as ministers we want to teach these things and help God's people step into the inheritance prepared for them, then we must fully surrender ourselves to the Holy Spirit's leading. In faith, we must claim the very life Christ lived on earth, trusting that the same Spirit who filled Him with the Word and with prayer will also do this in us.

Let's believe that the Spirit in us is the Spirit of Jesus—and that He is here to make us true sharers in His life. If we believe this and set our hearts on it, we will see a change in how we relate to the Word and prayer that we never imagined possible. Believe it firmly. Expect it confidently.

We know the vision of the valley of dry bones. The Lord told the prophet: "Prophesy to these bones... I will put breath in you, and you will live." (Ezekiel 37:4–5) When he spoke that first prophecy, the bones came together, flesh appeared, skin covered them—but there was no breath in them.

Preaching—the prophesying to the bones—had a powerful effect. It formed something new and promising, but it did not give life. Then God said: "Prophesy to the breath... Come from the four winds, breath, and breathe into these slain so that they may live." (verse 9)

When the prophet prayed this, the Spirit came, and the bodies came to life and stood up—a vast army.

Preaching created the form. Prayer brought the life.

Isn't much of our ministry exactly this—prophesying to dry bones? We preach God's promises. We call people to repentance. We see outward changes: more regular attendance, more interest, more seriousness. But still, in many cases: "There is no life in them."

Preaching must be followed by prayer. The preacher must see that preaching alone cannot bring real spiritual life. They must take time to pray—continually, persistently, urgently.

According to Scripture, we must work, struggle, and persevere in prayer. We must take no rest—and give God no rest—until He pours out the Spirit in overflowing power.

Do you feel it? A change must come in our work.

We must learn from Peter to continue in prayer as part of our ministry of the Word. As passionately as we preach, we must pray with equal passion. Like Paul, we must pray without ceasing. For the prayer "Come, breathe on these slain," the answer is certain.

WHOLEHEARTEDNESS

Life itself teaches us that if someone works at something without giving themselves to it wholeheartedly, they rarely succeed. Think of a student and their studies, a teacher, a businessperson, or a soldier.

Anyone who doesn't throw themselves fully into what they're doing almost always comes up short.

This is even more true in spiritual life—especially in the high and holy calling of speaking with a holy God in prayer and living in a way that pleases Him.

This is why God has said with such emphasis: "You will seek Me and find Me when you search for Me with all your heart" (Jeremiah 29:13).

And why God's servants have prayed: "I seek You with all my heart" (Psalm 119:10).

Have you ever stopped to consider how many Christians clearly do not seek God with their whole heart?

When they were troubled over their sins, they seemed to seek Him with all their heart. But once they knew they were forgiven, their lives showed they were religious, yes—but no one would look at them and say, "This person has given themselves completely to follow God and to serve Him as the central purpose of their life."

How is it with you? What does your own heart say? You may be someone who has thrown yourself wholeheartedly into your ministry—working faithfully, diligently, even passionately. Yet you might also have to admit: "My unsatisfactory prayer life comes from one thing—I haven't lived with a wholehearted surrender of everything that might keep me from fellowship with God."

This is a deeply serious question to bring into the inner chamber and to answer honestly before God. It's important to come to a clear conclusion—and to speak it openly to Him.

Prayerlessness can't be defeated as a stand-alone issue. It is directly tied to the state of your heart. Real prayer depends on an undivided heart. But you cannot create that undivided heart in yourself. You cannot make yourself able to say, "I seek God with all my heart." That is impossible for you—but God can do it.

"I will give them one heart to know Me" (Jeremiah 24:7).

"I will write My law on their hearts" (Jeremiah 31:33; Hebrews 8:10).

These promises awaken desire in us. And even if your desire feels weak, if there is a sincere willingness to pursue what God offers, then He will work in your heart—giving you both the desire and the ability.

It is one of the Holy Spirit's greatest works in us to make us willing and able to seek God with our whole heart.

Shouldn't we feel some shame when we think of how eagerly we give ourselves to earthly things—with all our heart and strength—yet when it comes to fellowship with our glorious God, we respond so little? We haven't sought Him with our whole heart.

12
"Follow Me"

Jesus didn't say "Follow Me" to everyone who believed in Him or hoped for His help. These words were for those He intended to make fishers of people. He repeated this calling later to Peter: "From now on you will be catching people" (Luke 5:10).

The holy work of loving souls and leading them to Christ can only be learned through close, steady fellowship with Him.

This is a powerful lesson for ministers, Christian workers, and anyone who wants to influence others spiritually. Jesus invited His disciples into constant nearness with Him. Mark 3:14 says, "He appointed twelve so that they might be with Him, and that He might send them out to preach."

On His final night He said, "You also will testify, because you have been with Me from the beginning" (John 15:27).

Even outsiders could see this fellowship: "You were with Jesus," a woman said to Peter (Matthew 26:71). And in the Sanhedrin, they recognized that the apostles "had been with Jesus" (Acts 4:13).

The defining qualification for anyone who wants to witness for Christ is this: they have been with Him. Ongoing fellowship with Jesus is the only real training for becoming a minister of the Holy Spirit. This is the challenge—and privilege—of every minister. Only those who follow the Lord wholeheartedly, like Caleb, can teach others to follow Him.

And what grace this is—that Jesus Himself trains us to become like Him, so others can learn from us. Like Paul said: "You became imitators of us and of the Lord..." (1 Thessalonians 1:6). "Imitate me, as I imitate Christ" (1 Corinthians 11:1).

There has never been a teacher who works as patiently with His students as Jesus does with those who preach His word. No effort is too great for Him. He will shape us, teach us, correct us, sanctify us, and prepare us for His work—just as surely as the love that took Him to the cross.

So how can we ever say that spending time in prayer is "too much"? Will we not gladly give ourselves fully to the One who gave everything for us? Will we not see it as our greatest joy to meet with Him every day in fellowship?

All who long for blessing in ministry must hear His call: "Be with Me." Let this be your deepest joy. It will also be the strongest foundation for fruitful service.

O Lord, draw me, hold me, and teach me to live each day in fellowship with You by faith.

THE HOLY TRINITY

God is an endless fountain of love and blessing. Christ is the reservoir where God's fullness was made visible and opened to us. The Holy Spirit is the living stream flowing from the Father and the Son to the world. And we, God's redeemed children, are the channels through which His love, grace, and power flow to others.

This gives us a glimpse of the astonishing place God calls us into: partnering with Him as distributors of His grace.

Prayer that focuses only on our own needs is just the beginning. The true glory of prayer is intercession—

bringing Christ's grace and the Spirit's power to people still in darkness.

The more a channel stays connected to the reservoir, the more freely the water flows. Likewise, the more our hearts stay occupied with Christ's fullness and the Spirit's work, the more joyful and strong our lives become.

But even this is only preparation. The more time we give to fellowship with the Father, Son, and Holy Spirit, the more courage and ability we receive to pray blessing down on souls, on ministers, and on the Church.

Ask yourself: Am I really a channel that stays open so living water can flow through me to thirsty people?

Have I fully offered myself to God to carry the Spirit's life-giving work to others?

Have I experienced so little power in prayer because I've focused almost entirely on myself?

Your new prayer life in Christ will grow only as you learn to intercede—laboring in prayer for others so they may come to know Him.

Spend time meditating on this picture: God, the ever-flowing fountain of love; Christ, the fullness of grace; the Spirit, the living stream; and you—a channel through which heaven touches earth every day.

LIFE AND PRAYER

Our life shapes our prayer, and our prayer shapes our life. Every person is constantly "praying" in some sense—reaching toward the world, toward comfort, toward success, toward whatever seems to promise satisfaction. These inner desires can be so loud that even when someone speaks words of prayer to God, He may not "hear" them, because the heart is crying out for something else entirely.

A life driven by the world or by self-centered motives

makes prayer weak and keeps answers at a distance. For many Christians, there's a battle between their lifestyle and their prayer life—and the lifestyle wins.

But prayer can also reshape life. If I give myself fully to God in prayer, prayer will begin to push back against the flesh and sin. Prayer can govern my entire life because prayer brings Jesus and the Holy Spirit into every part of it, cleansing and renewing it.

Many people try to "work themselves up" to pray more, even though their spiritual life is weak. They don't realize the reverse is true: only as spiritual life grows strong will prayer grow strong.

Prayer and life are deeply connected. Ask yourself: Which speaks louder in you—five or ten minutes of prayer, or an entire day filled with desires for other things?

Don't be surprised if some prayers go unanswered. Your life and prayer may be working against each other. Your heart may be more devoted to daily living than to communion with God.

Learn this key principle: My prayer must direct my whole life. What I ask from God isn't decided only during a brief prayer time. I need a prayer that involves my whole heart. What I desire from God must carry through the day—then my prayer has room to grow and receive an answer.

When prayer takes hold of my life, it keeps me aware of God all day long. Then I can honestly say, "I wait for You all day long" (Psalm 25:5).

Let's not only think about how much time we spend praying, but also how much our prayer shapes the rest of our lives.

Perseverance in Prayer

The apostles said, "It wouldn't be right for us to give up preaching the word of God to wait on tables" (Acts 6:2).

Deacons were appointed so the apostles could remain focused on the two main callings of ministry: prayer and the ministry of the word (Acts 6:4).

Dr. Alexander Whyte once said that every time he received his salary, he felt the deacons had done their part faithfully—but he had to ask whether he had been equally faithful in prayer and the ministry of the word.

Another minister commented, "People would be shocked if I announced I was dividing my time equally—half for prayer, half for preaching."

But this is exactly what Peter lived. He went up on the roof to pray, and there God gave him clarity about his mission to the Gentiles. There the men from Cornelius arrived. There the Spirit said, "Go with them without hesitation" (Acts 10:19–20). And from that place of prayer he walked into one of the biggest breakthroughs in the early Church—the outpouring of the Spirit on the Gentiles. Prayer gave him direction, confidence, boldness, and clarity. This is what perseverance in prayer produces.

Have you ever seriously considered why you receive a salary, a home, and freedom from secular work? It's so you can devote yourself to prayer and the ministry of the word. This is your power. This is your wisdom. This is the fountain of blessing for your people.

No wonder spiritual life is often weak when the most important work—persevering prayer—doesn't hold first place.

Peter acted as he did because he was full of the Spirit. We must not settle for anything less than full surrender to the Spirit's leadership.

Only then can we say, "God has made us competent as ministers of the Spirit" (2 Corinthians 3:6).

Carnal or Spiritual?

There's a major difference between a spiritual Christian and a carnal (flesh-driven) one, though many overlook it.

A spiritual Christian is someone who walks by the Spirit and has crucified the flesh (Galatians 5:24).

A carnal Christian lives by what the flesh wants and tries to satisfy it (Romans 13:14).

The Galatians began their Christian life in the Spirit but drifted into the flesh. Yet among them were some who were spiritual—people who could gently restore those who had wandered.

Paul saw the same thing in Corinth: believers who were saved, active, and gifted, but still carnal (1 Corinthians 3:1–3).

A carnal Christian may be passionate, active, religious, and sincere—but much of it happens in their own strength.

A spiritual Christian lives by surrender to the Spirit, deep dependence on Christ, and constant fellowship with Him.

It's vital for each of us to honestly ask: Am I spiritual or carnal?

A minister can be completely orthodox and deeply committed to ministry, yet still operate mostly from human effort. One of the clearest signs of this is a weak prayer life. A spiritual person delights in prayer and perseveres in it; the Spirit inspires prayer.

The shift from carnal to spiritual doesn't make sense to the carnal person at first. They don't know how it could happen. But as God opens their eyes, they realize it's impossible without Him.

This awakening leads them into prayer, quietness before God, meditation on His word, and a surrender that abandons all confidence in their own strength.

On that path, God gives faith: God can. God is willing. God will do it. A soul that clings to Jesus will be led by the Spirit into this confidence.

How can you say to others, "I couldn't speak to you as spiritual people, but as people of the flesh" (1 Corinthians 3:1)? Only if you've personally experienced God leading you out of carnality and into spiritual life.

And He will teach you. Just persevere in prayer and faith.

13

GEORGE MÜLLER; HUDSON TAYLOR; LIGHT FROM THE INNER CHAMBER

God has given the church many examples of what a life of prayer can accomplish. The apostle Paul is one of them. In more recent history, George Müller stands out as living proof that God still answers prayer in literal, practical, astonishing ways.

Müller didn't just receive more than a million pounds over the course of his life for the support of his orphanages —he also said he believed God had given him more than thirty thousand souls in answer to prayer. Some of those were people he prayed for every day for more than fifty years, convinced God would save them.

When asked why he felt so sure his prayers would be answered, he described five things he always tried to observe:

He prayed according to God's will. He never doubted that God wanted the people he prayed for to be saved, because Scripture says God "desires all people to be saved and to come to the knowledge of the truth" (1 Timothy 2:4). And "If we ask anything according to His will, He hears us" (1 John 5:14).

He prayed in Jesus' name, not his own. He relied entirely on the worthiness of Christ, not on himself (John 14:14).

He believed God would hear him. He took Jesus' words seriously: "Whatever you ask for in prayer, believe that you have received it, and it will be yours" (Mark 11:24).

He kept his conscience clean. He avoided known sin, remembering, "If I had cherished sin in my heart, the Lord would not have listened" (Psalm 66:18).

He persevered. He kept praying—even for more than fifty years—because Jesus said God will answer those who "cry out to Him day and night" (Luke 18:7).

Müller's approach wasn't complicated. It was simply fellowship with God in prayer until he knew, by faith, that God had heard him. The path Müller walked is open to us all.

Hudson Taylor

When Hudson Taylor surrendered himself completely to God as a young man, he felt a strong call to China. Influenced by the story of George Müller, he began to ask the Lord to teach him to trust God for everything.

He believed that if he was going to live by faith in China, he must learn to live by faith first in England. So he prayed that God would help him rely on Him for his income rather than asking directly for his salary as a doctor's assistant. The doctor he worked with was kind but forgetful, often failing to pay on time. This created real struggle—and real lessons.

Taylor believed Romans 13:8, "Owe no one anything," should be taken literally. He refused to go into debt. This forced him to depend fully on God and taught him what later became one of the great principles of his ministry:

"Move people through God." Instead of urging people directly, he made his needs known to God and trusted God to move others to act.

This principle shaped everything: the conversion of the Chinese, the support of the mission, the calling of new missionaries, and his own day-to-day provision.

Years later, while in China, he prayed that God would provide twenty-four missionaries, two for each unreached province. God answered that prayer—but there was no mission society to send them. He knew God could support him personally, but he wrestled with whether those twenty-four would live by the same faith. The pressure of this question made him seriously ill.

Eventually, he realized God could take care of twenty-four people as easily as one. That breakthrough freed him. He accepted the responsibility in faith, and God led him step by step through many difficult tests into deeper trust.

Those original twenty-four missionaries eventually grew into a movement of more than a thousand, all relying on God for support. Many mission societies later acknowledged how much they learned from Hudson Taylor's example—particularly the principle: Faith may rely on God to move people to accomplish what His children have asked Him in prayer.

If you want to go deeper into the story, read *Hudson Taylor's Early Years* by Dr. and Mrs. Howard Taylor. The book is full of rich lessons about walking with God in the inner chamber and serving Him in mission work.

Light From the Inner Chamber

"When you pray, go into your private room, shut your door, and pray to your Father who is in secret. And your Father who sees in secret will reward you." — Matthew 6:6

Jesus had just warned His disciples about two kinds of empty prayer: the prayer of hypocrites who want to impress people, and the prayer of unbelievers who think many words will make God listen.

Both misunderstand what prayer actually is. Prayer only has value because it is addressed to a personal God who sees, hears, and responds.

In this verse, Jesus teaches a profound lesson about the privilege we have in the secret place—the inner room. To understand it, we need to see what the inner chamber reveals:

1. THE WONDERFUL LOVE OF GOD

Think about who God is: His greatness, His holiness, His glory—and then think about the privilege He offers His children. Every one of us, no matter how weak or sinful, is invited to come to Him any hour of the day and talk with Him freely, for as long as we want.

Whenever we enter the inner room, God is ready to meet us. He offers fellowship, strength, joy, and the deep assurance that He is with us and will take up our concerns as His own. He even promises to bless our work and daily life with the results of what we ask Him in secret.

Shouldn't this invitation fill us with joy? What an honor. What a source of help. What a place of rest for every need.

Whether we're overwhelmed, have fallen into sin, are seeking spiritual growth, praying for our families, praying for our church, or even praying for the world—this promise covers everything: "Pray to your Father who is in secret; He will reward you."

If we understood this, no place on earth would feel more inviting than the inner room. The joy of a child with a loving father, a friend with a generous benefactor, or a citizen with open access to a king—all these pale in comparison to the privilege of meeting with God Himself.

In the inner chamber, you can speak with God as long and as honestly as you wish, knowing He is truly there with you.

Let's thank God daily that He has given us such a gift—an inner room where His love is poured out in ways perfectly suited to our needs.

2. The Deep Sinfulness of Human Nature

With such an incredible invitation, you might expect every believer to run joyfully to the inner chamber every day. But the reality? All over the world there is a common confession: private prayer is neglected.

Some Christians make almost no use of the secret place. They attend church and identify as believers, but they know little about personal fellowship with God.

Others use it only briefly or out of habit—mostly to ease the conscience—so they seldom experience joy or refreshing in prayer.

Even those who know something of its blessing often admit that they struggle to maintain regular, daily fellowship with the Father, as naturally and consistently as they eat their daily bread.

Why is the inner chamber so often powerless in our lives?

Because our fallen nature resists God.

Because the world feels more attractive than being alone with Him.

Because we forget Scripture's clear warning that "the flesh is hostile to God" (Romans 8:7).

Because we walk more in the flesh than in the Spirit, so the Spirit cannot strengthen us in prayer.

And because we let Satan steal the weapon of prayer from our hands—leaving us weak in the face of temptation.

The deepest evidence of our sinful nature may be this: we ignore or lightly treat God's incredible invitation to meet with Him in secret.

Even Christ's ministers confess that they know they pray too little. They know Scripture says their true power is found in prayer—that only prayer can clothe them with power from on high for real fruitfulness.

Yet the world's demands and the pull of the flesh distract them. They work passionately, but neglect the one thing most necessary. And without it, they cannot receive the essential gift of the Holy Spirit in their ministry.

May God give us grace to see, in the light of the inner chamber, the true depth of our own need—and the astonishing love that still invites us to come.

3. The Glorious Grace of Christ Jesus

Is there any hope for real change? Are we doomed to stay this way? Thank God—there is hope.

The One who calls us into the inner chamber is the same Lord Jesus who saves us from all sin. He is both able and willing to set us free from the sin of prayerlessness. He didn't redeem us from every other sin only to leave this one for us to overcome in our own strength. No—here too, He invites us to come to Him and say: "Lord, if You are willing, You can make me clean." "I do believe; help my unbelief."

How then can we experience this deliverance?

The way is the same way every sinner must come to Christ. Begin by admitting, honestly and simply, that you have neglected the inner room. Confess it before Him. Bow in humility and sorrow.

Tell Him how your own heart misled you—how you assumed you could pray well enough on your own.

Tell Him how the weakness of your flesh, the pull of the world, and confidence in yourself led you away from prayer.

Acknowledge that you have no strength to fix this.

Do this sincerely. You cannot correct this by willpower or effort. Instead, come into the inner room in your sin and

The Prayer Life

weakness. And there, begin to thank God—perhaps more deeply than you ever have—that the grace of Jesus truly can make it possible for you to speak with your Father as a child should.

Surrender to Him again: your sin, your weakness, your whole heart, your whole will. Give it all to Him so He may cleanse you, take possession of you, and rule your life as His own.

Even if your heart feels cold and lifeless, keep choosing faith. Trust that Christ is both almighty and faithful.

If you do, deliverance will come. Expect it.

Then you will begin to understand that the inner chamber is not a place where you try to do the impossible. It is the place where Jesus' glorious grace makes possible what you could never do on your own—true fellowship with God, and the desire and strength to walk with Him day by day.

14

THE CROSS-SPIRIT IN OUR LORD

We often seek the Spirit's work so we can have more power, more love, more holiness, more insight into Scripture, or clearer direction. But all of these are secondary.

God's great purpose in giving the Spirit is to reveal and glorify Jesus Himself in us.

The risen, heavenly Christ must become a living, present reality—someone we know, trust, and walk with every day. Our earthly life is meant to be lived in steady, unbroken fellowship with Him.

This is the Spirit's primary work: to make Christ the very life of our lives. God wants to strengthen us inwardly through His Spirit so Christ will truly dwell in our hearts, filling us with His love until we overflow with God's fullness.

This was the secret of the disciples' joy. They received again—into their hearts—the Jesus they thought they had lost. This prepared them for Pentecost. They were absorbed with Him. He was everything to them.

Their hearts were emptied of all else so the Spirit could fill them with Christ. And in that fullness, they had power for the life and service Jesus asked of them.

Is this our goal too? Is this what we truly want in our prayers, our desires, and our daily experience?

Lord, teach us that the blessing we long for can only be

kept and deepened through daily, intimate fellowship with You in the secret place.

A Deeper Secret of Pentecost

It seems to me there is a deeper key to Pentecost we often overlook. We think about Jesus in heavenly glory— seated at the Father's throne, full of majesty and love. But we forget that in heaven He is still known first as the crucified one. "I saw… a Lamb standing, as though slain" (Revelation 5:6).

He is worshipped because of the cross. It is His highest glory. And it is as the crucified one that He reigns. So it is essential that we learn to know Him this way on earth— as the crucified Lord so His heart, His character, and His cross-shaped life may be seen in us, and so others may meet Him through us.

I am convinced that because the cross is Christ's highest glory, and because the Spirit's greatest work was strengthening Him to offer Himself to God, the Spirit's greatest work in us is to bring us into fellowship with Christ in His cross—to form in us the same cross-shaped spirit we see in Him.

And here is the piercing question that began to rise in my heart: Could it be that our prayers for the Spirit's power have gone unanswered because we have sought the Spirit too little for this purpose—to make us like the crucified Christ?

This is the heart of Pentecost:

The Spirit comes from the cross.

He comes from the Father who delighted in Christ's humility, obedience, and self-giving.

He comes from the Son who received the Spirit's fullness because He poured Himself out.

He comes to reveal to us the crucified Christ who stands

at the center of the throne.

He comes to give us the crucified Christ's life, so we can truly say: "I have been crucified with Christ; and I no longer live, but Christ lives in me."

To understand this, we must pause and consider the meaning and value of the cross.

We must look at the cross from two sides.

1. What the cross accomplished

The cross removes sin and breaks its power. This is its message to the sinner: full and free deliverance.

2. The spirit of the cross

This is the message for those who follow Christ.

Philippians 2:8 captures it: He humbled Himself to the lowest place. He obeyed completely—nothing held back. He sacrificed Himself entirely, even to death on a cross.

These three—humility, obedience, self-sacrifice—reveal the perfection of Christ's heart. This is why the Father exalted Him, and why heaven adores Him. This is why He is the Lamb at the center of the throne.

THE SPIRIT OF THE CROSS IN US

Everything Christ is, He desires to be in us. The spirit of the cross was His glory—and He intends it to be ours.

He wants to shape His likeness in us. He wants us to share His life. So Paul writes:

"Let this mind be in you which was also in Christ Jesus." "We have the mind of Christ."

The fellowship of the cross isn't just a duty—it is a privilege. The Holy Spirit makes this possible. He takes what belongs to Christ and brings it into our hearts.

15
TAKING UP THE CROSS

When Jesus told His disciples to "take up their cross," they could not yet understand what He meant. But He was preparing them for the day they would see Him carrying His cross.

From His baptism onward, Jesus carried the cross in His heart. He lived constantly aware that He bore the sentence of death for sin, and He would carry it to the end.

The disciples slowly learned that taking up the cross meant embracing this truth: "My old life is under a death sentence. I must continually surrender my sinful nature to that death."

As they watched Him, they began to understand the cross was the only true power that could free them from sin—and that they must receive from Him the real spirit of the cross:

- humility in their weakness
- obedience that lays down their own will
- self-denial that refuses to serve the flesh or please the world

"Take up your cross and follow Me" became the call that prepared them for His life to become theirs.

CRUCIFIED WITH CHRIST

After Christ died and rose, Paul expressed this truth clearly: "I have been crucified with Christ." "I will never boast except in the cross of our Lord Jesus Christ."

Paul teaches that every believer must live as someone crucified with Christ. Christ lives in us as the crucified Christ, forming in us the spirit of the cross.

He says our "old self was crucified with Him." Those who belong to Christ "have crucified the flesh."
We died with Him, and therefore we must count ourselves dead to sin and alive to God.

Only the soul that lives continually in the fellowship of the cross can walk closely with Christ and glory in His nearness.

THE FELLOWSHIP OF THE CROSS

Many Christians trust the cross for forgiveness but know little of the cross as a daily fellowship. They rely on its benefits but don't seek fellowship with the crucified Lord Himself.

But the cross is meant to draw us into daily heart-fellowship with Jesus—the Lamb at the center of the throne.

This is not only possible—it is God's purpose. Pentecost itself proves it. The Spirit was given to make the glorified, crucified Christ present with us in our earthly lives.

Let's explore this more in the reflections ahead.

16
THE HOLY SPIRIT AND THE CROSS

The Holy Spirit always leads us to the cross.

We see this in Jesus. The Spirit taught Him and strengthened Him to offer Himself without defect to God. We see it in the disciples. When they were filled with the Spirit, He led them to preach Christ as the crucified One. Later, He also led them to rejoice in sharing the sufferings of Christ, counting it an honor to suffer for His name.

And the cross, in turn, always sends us back to the Spirit.

When Christ had borne the cross, He received the Spirit from the Father so that He might pour Him out.

When the three thousand bowed before the crucified Christ at Pentecost, they received the promised Holy Spirit. When the disciples rejoiced that they were counted worthy to suffer shame for His name, they were again filled afresh with the Spirit.

The bond between the Spirit and the cross cannot be broken. They belong together always. We see this very clearly in Paul's letters:

"Jesus Christ was clearly portrayed as crucified... Did you receive the Spirit by works of the law or by hearing with faith?" (Galatians 3:1–2)

"Christ redeemed us from the curse of the law... so that we might receive the promise of the Spirit through faith." (Galatians 3:13–14)

"God sent His Son... to redeem those under the law... God has sent the Spirit of His Son into our hearts." (Galatians 4:4–6)

"Those who belong to Christ Jesus have crucified the flesh with its passions and desires... If we live by the Spirit, let us also keep in step with the Spirit." (Galatians 5:24–25)

"You also were put to death in relation to the law through the body of Christ... so that we may serve in the new way of the Spirit." (Romans 7:4–6)

"The law of the Spirit of life in Christ Jesus has set you free from the law of sin and death... God condemned sin in the flesh so that the law's requirement would be fulfilled in us who walk not according to the flesh but according to the Spirit." (Romans 8:2–4)

Everywhere, the Spirit and the cross go together—even in heaven.

In Revelation, John sees "a Lamb, standing as though it had been slain," and this Lamb has "seven eyes, which are the seven Spirits of God sent into all the earth" (Revelation 5:6). Later, he sees "the river of the water of life" (clearly a picture of the Holy Spirit), "flowing from the throne of God and of the Lamb" (Revelation 22:1).

Think also of the rock Moses struck in the wilderness. When it was struck, water flowed out and the people drank. In the same way, when Christ—the true Rock—was struck at the cross and then took His place as the slain Lamb on the throne, the fullness of the Holy Spirit began to flow from the throne of God and of the Lamb to the whole world.

It is useless to pray for fullness of the Spirit if we are not willing to come under the full power of the cross.

Think again of the one hundred twenty disciples. The crucifixion had broken and seized hold of their hearts. They could talk about nothing but the crucified Lord.

When He showed them His hands and feet and said, "Receive the Holy Spirit" (John 20:22), their hearts were full of the cross.

So when He ascended and they waited in the upper room, their hearts were full of the crucified and risen Christ. They were ready to be filled with the Spirit.

Then they were able to preach boldly: "Repent and believe in the crucified One"—and the Holy Spirit was poured out.

Christ gave Himself to the cross completely. The disciples also surrendered themselves completely. The cross asks the same from us. It lays claim to our whole life.

To agree to this requires both a deep decision of our will (which we are too weak to make on our own) and a powerful act of God (which He is ready to work when we throw ourselves helplessly and honestly into His hands).

THE SPIRIT AND THE CROSS

Why are there not more men and women who can joyfully testify that the Holy Spirit has taken possession of them and given them new power to witness?

Why so few who can say, from experience, that the Spirit has filled them?

We cannot avoid this searching question: What is blocking the way?

The Father is more willing to give the Holy Spirit than earthly parents are to give bread to their children. Yet the lack of power in the church remains. Is the Spirit at fault? Of course not.

Most of us would admit the problem lies here: The church is too much under the power of the flesh and the world. We understand too little of the cutting, searching power of the cross. So the Spirit does not find many vessels that are ready to be filled.

Some say that all this is too deep or too high for them. But that only shows how little we have taken seriously what Christ and Paul teach about the cross.

Here is good news: The Spirit who is already in you—even if you feel His work is small—wants to become your Teacher. He wants to lead you to the cross and show you what the crucified Christ can do for you and in you.

But He needs your time. He needs you to slow down enough for Him to reveal these things in the inner chamber.

He wants to show you how neglect of the secret place has held you back from fellowship with Christ, from knowledge of the cross, and from the Spirit's power.

He wants to teach you what it means to deny yourself, to take up your cross, to lose your life for Christ's sake, and to follow Him.

You may feel ignorant and spiritually dull, but He is able and willing to take you in hand and open up the secret of the spiritual life far beyond what you imagine.

Start at the beginning. Be faithful in the inner chamber. Thank God that you can count on the Spirit to meet you there.

Even if everything feels cold, dry, and strained, bow quietly before the Lord Jesus, who longs for you. Thank the Father that He has already given you the Spirit. Be sure of this: everything you still need to learn about the flesh, the world, and the cross—the Spirit of Christ in you is ready to teach you.

Believe this is for you. Christ belongs fully to you, and He longs to take full possession of you. He can and will do this through the Holy Spirit. But for that, time is necessary.

Give Him time each day in the secret place. You can be certain He will keep His promise: "The one who has My commands and keeps them is the one who loves Me. And the one who loves Me will be loved by My Father. I also will love him and will reveal Myself to him." (John 14:21)

Persevere—not only in praying for yourself, but also for your church, your leaders, all believers, and the whole body of Christ. Ask God to strengthen them with power through His Spirit, so that Christ may live in their hearts by faith.

Blessed will be the day when the answer comes—and the Spirit reveals and glorifies Christ and His cross among us as the Lamb slain, standing at the center of the throne.

THE CROSS AND THE FLESH

The cross and "the flesh" are enemies. The cross wants to condemn and put the flesh to death. The flesh wants to reject, ignore, and overthrow the cross.

When we hear that the cross is the necessary preparation for fullness of the Spirit, many of us will also discover how much in us still needs to be crucified.

We must see that our whole fallen nature is under a death sentence, and that it must be brought to death by the cross so that Christ's new life can fully rule in us.

We must see our nature's corruption and hostility to God clearly enough that we want to be freed from it completely. We must come to say with Paul: "Nothing good lives in me, that is, in my flesh" (Romans 7:18).

"The mindset of the flesh is hostile to God... it cannot submit to God's law" (Romans 8:7).

This is what the flesh is at its core: it hates God and His holy law.

Here is the wonder of redemption: Christ bore the judgment and curse of God against the flesh on the cross and nailed it there forever.

If we believe what God says about the cursed mind of

the flesh, and we long to be delivered from it, we will begin to love the cross as our only way of escape.

"Our old self was crucified with Him" (Romans 6:6).

"Those who belong to Christ Jesus have crucified the flesh" (Galatians 5:24).

Those who belong to Christ choose to treat the flesh as God's enemy and their own enemy, and to regard it as nailed with Christ to the cross. This is part of the eternal redemption Christ has brought us.

We cannot achieve this by thinking hard enough or trying hard enough. It is something Christ teaches us and gives us as we stay close to Him day by day and receive everything from Him. It is something the Holy Spirit makes real in us—giving us victory over the flesh by the power of the cross.

THE CROSS AND THE WORLD

What the flesh is in the small circle of our own hearts, the world is in the large circle of human life.

"The flesh" and "the world" are two expressions of the same dark power, ruled by "the god of this world."

When the cross deals with the flesh as cursed, we begin to see what the world really is.

Jesus said of the world, "They hated Me and My Father" (John 15:24), and this hatred was proved at the cross. But through that same cross Christ won the victory and broke the world's power over us. So Paul can say: "I will never boast about anything except the cross of our Lord Jesus Christ. Through Him the world has been crucified to me, and I to the world" (Galatians 6:14).

The cross was for Paul a daily reality: in what he suffered from the world, and in the victory he had over it.

John says, "The whole world is under the sway of the

evil one" (1 John 5:19), and yet he also says: "Who is the one who conquers the world but the one who believes that Jesus is the Son of God? This is the One who came by water and blood—Jesus Christ… And the Spirit is the One who testifies" (1 John 5:5–6).

Against the two great powers of the enemy—the flesh and the world—God has given us two great powers from heaven: the cross and the Spirit.

Christ won His greatest victory with His hands and feet nailed to the cross. We remain safe in God's shelter only as long as we remain under the shadow of that cross.

The cross must be our home. Only there are we truly protected.

17

A Testimony & An Epilogue

A Testimony

The following thoughts, adapted from Starlight by G. Sterrenberg, express the truth of the cross in simple and powerful words. They connect closely with what has been said about "The Fellowship of the Cross" and "The Holy Spirit and the Cross."

Christ, our Head, took the lowest place on the cross. He has marked out that same lowest place for us, His members.

The brightness of God's glory (Hebrews 1:3) became the One rejected by people (Isaiah 53:3). Since then, the only real "right" we have is to be last and least. Whenever we demand more than that, we show that we have not yet understood the cross.

We long for a "higher" life. We will find it only as we sink deeper into fellowship with Christ in His cross.

God has given the crucified One the highest place in heaven (Revelation 5). Shouldn't we also give Him the highest place in our hearts? We do that when we live, moment by moment, as people crucified with Him (Galatians 2:19–20). In this way we honor the crucified Lord.

The Lamb won His greatest victory with His hands and feet nailed. We stay in the shadow of the Almighty only as long as we stay under the shadow of the cross. The cross must become our dwelling place. There we are safe.

We only understand our own cross when we begin to understand His. We want to come so close to it that we not only look at it but also touch it—and even more, that we take it up. Then the cross becomes an inward reality.

When this happens, the cross begins to work in us. We experience its power in this: that we do not faint under it but carry it with joy.

What would Jesus be, in our eyes, without His cross? His pierced feet crushed the enemy's head, and His pierced hands stripped him of his weapons (Matthew 12:29).

What are we without the cross? Don't let it go. Hold it fast.

Do we imagine we can walk a different road than He walked? Many believers make almost no progress simply because they refuse to take up the cross.

Epilogue

Let me say a final word about the attitude of heart this book calls for.

It is not enough to understand the ideas, agree with them, and feel pleased with the insight you've gained. Something more is needed.

You must be ready to surrender yourself to the truth—to be willing, with an undivided will, to do at once all that you see to be God's will.

A book like this, which deals with prayer and hidden fellowship with God, is only useful when we are prepared to receive and obey everything that we recognize as God's word for us.

If this readiness is lacking, knowledge will actually

harden us and make it harder to receive more life later on.

Satan tries hard to gain control over the believer's inner chamber. He knows that if there is unfaithfulness in prayer, Christian service will have little real power. We may preach, teach, and work, but without persevering prayer there will be little fruit.

Many of us, and many in the wider church, face the same burning question:

Will we truly fight to win back the weapon of believing prayer that Satan has partly taken from us?

Everything depends on this—especially for ministers of the gospel. Their calling is to be people of prayer, clothed each day in the inner room with power from on high.

We, together with the church throughout the world, have to admit that prayer does not hold its rightful place in our life with God—certainly not the place God's word and promise give it, nor the place our present need demands.

Public rededication at conferences is not difficult.
What is difficult is maintaining that surrender when old habits and the power of the flesh try to pull us back.
Faith is still weak; it will take struggle and sacrifice to overcome the enemy in Christ's name.

Our churches are battlefields. Satan uses all his strength to prevent us from becoming people of prayer—people through whom God can win victories in heaven and on earth.

So much depends on this: for us personally, for our congregations, and for God's kingdom.

It is with this in mind, and with a deep sense of my own unworthiness, that I have written these pages—praying that they might help brothers and sisters in this battle.

I have asked the Lord to give this book a place in many inner chambers, and to help every reader who sees God's will in it to respond at once in obedience.

In wartime, everything depends on each soldier obeying the word of command, even if it costs their life.

In our conflict with Satan, we will not overcome unless each of us is ready—even while reading this simple book—to say from the heart:

"What God shows me, I will do. When I see something is His will, I will accept it and act on it immediately."

Everything depends on this spirit of surrender and instant obedience.

May God, in His great grace, use this book as a bond of fellowship, so that we may think of one another, pray for one another, and strengthen one another in the battle of prayer—until the enemy is driven back, and the life of God is powerfully revealed among His people.

www.ingramcontent.com/pod-product-compliance
Lightning Source LLC
Chambersburg PA
CBHW030331080526
44584CB00012B/811